Sewing PRETTY LITTLE Accessories

Charming Projects to Make and Give

Sewing PRETTY LITTLE Accessories

Charming Projects to Make and Give

CHERIE LEE

an Imprint of Fox Chapel Publishing
www.d-originals.com

A word of thanks to my editor

This project has represented a new set of challenges and obstacles that I could not have overcome without my editor. Thank you for your trust, inspiration and careful design of this book. Thank you also for your hard work and for sharing this experience with me not only as an editor, but also as a friend. This book is not just mine, but is a result of our hard work together.

Handmade Gifts: 38 Projects of Remnants (手作小確幸。禮物組！：美布無剩超完美提案！)
by Cherie Lee

Published by arrangement with SYSTEX CORPORATION through LEE's Literary Agency, Taiwan

Credits for the English Edition
Publisher: Carole Giagnocavo
Acquisition Editor: Peg Couch
Editor: Colleen Dorsey
Designer: Ashley Millhouse

ISBN 978-1-57421-861-9

Sewing Pretty Little Accessories is a revised and abridged translation of the original Chinese book. This version published by New Design Originals, an imprint of Fox Chapel Publishing Company, Inc., East Petersburg, PA.

Library of Congress Cataloging-in-Publication Data

Lee, Cherie.
[Shou zuo xiao que xing, li wu zu. Selections. English]
Sewing pretty little accessories / Cherie Lee.
pages cm
"Handmade gifts, 38 projects of remnants."
Includes index.
ISBN 978-1-57421-861-9 (alk. paper)
1. Textile crafts. 2. Sewing. 3. Dress accessories. I. Title.
TT699.L4645213 2014
646'.3--dc23
2013030528

Printed in China
First printing

About the Author

Cherie Lee has a long history of sewing and designing stunning handmade items in her native Taiwan. In 2006, Cherie established her own handmade brand, Love · Catmint, and began attending many creative design events and festivals, which she continues to participate in as both guest and presenter today. In 2008, Cherie began to focus her handmade projects on cozy accessories inspired by soft fabrics. Since starting her sewing journey, Cherie has been featured in the news and in several magazines, and has published two sewing books on indoor shoes. In 2012, she established Catmint Studio, where she spends her days working on her next batch of impressive projects. Through her brand Love · Catmint, Cherie shares the comfort and happiness of soft handmade goods with her customers, friends, and family.
www.lovecatmint.com

"I love to play around with small bits of fabric, I love the bliss of handmade projects, and, most of all, I love the satisfaction that you feel when you look upon your finished project."

Publisher's Note

When Taiwanese designer Cherie Lee set out to write this book on making small gifts, little did she know that her work would make its way to the United States. But that is precisely what happened: when we at Design Originals got the chance to look at her charming designs, we knew American readers would love them. So much so, in fact, that we have decided to publish two volumes of her work.

This book, the second volume, features a variety of accessories from hats, slippers, and coin purses to camera cases, card folios, and wallets. There is something for every taste and every function. Whether you are using fabric from your stash or buying fresh bundles from your local craft store, you'll adore the nineteen projects selected. And after you make all your favorites from this book, be sure to check out Cherie's first book, *Sewing Pretty Little Things*, which features bags and clutches to match any style or outfit.

Cherie joins the rapidly growing collection of talented craft authors from around the world selected for inclusion in the Design Originals line. Known for its innovative topics and highly regarded authors, Design Originals will continue to bring the best selections of foreign and American craft books to North American readers. We love these books, and we hope you will, too. Enjoy!

Carole

Carole Giagnocavo
Publisher
carole@d-originals.com

Editor's Note

Planning this project has been both a wonderful, enjoyable experience as well as a challenging and difficult journey. There are those inevitable times when you are painstakingly trying to come up with an idea, only to find yourself continuously hitting a brick wall; but such times are counteracted when you find inspiration for a great idea that makes you so excited that you could jump up and dance. I have been lucky enough to share these delights and hardships during this project with the book's author, Cherie Lee.

After Cherie finished her 2010 work on handmade indoor shoes, she wanted to strike again while the iron was hot, so she immediately set out to start on a new handmade project. Cherie and I began brainstorming until, after hours of throwing ideas back and forth, we came up with the idea of handmade gifts using fabric remnants.

The nineteen projects in this book appeal to a variety of different interests and needs. The author's key motive for this book is to reach out to a more diverse audience with the best yet of her cloth-work books. In creating this varied set of gifts, the most important issue that was resolved is one of the most common problems constantly presenting itself to handmade products: what do you do with your leftover scraps of material? Those last fragments of cloth left over after you have finished your other projects are perfect for the bags and accessories in this book.

I hope that you will find that each of these projects can help to serve as sincere and meaningful gifts for yourself or for those you love.

Table of Contents

51

46

Bags, Pouches, and Purses

78

81

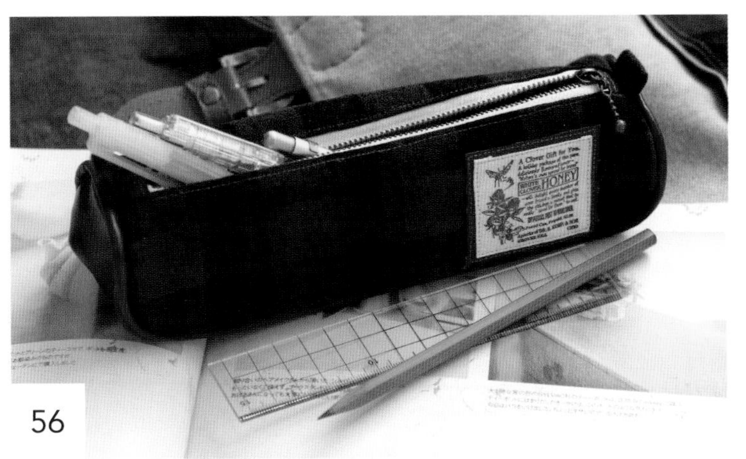

56

73

Cases and Covers

Accessories

84

86

102

Introduction

One afternoon, my editor and I began discussing our thoughts for a new book, and as we chatted and bounced ideas back and forth, we finally came up with a plan.

This book of gifts has many purposes. I find that it is often difficult to express your emotions to the people closest to you; however, a gift can help deliver your most earnest wishes directly into the hands of those you love. This is truly the origin of the gift of giving, which is one of the underlying themes of this book.

We often tend to take care of others while neglecting our own wants and needs. However, loving oneself is also very important, and it is only by being good and truthful to ourselves that we may truly be loved by the people around us. I challenge you to first give the gift of happiness to yourself in order to allow your own heart to fill with contentment and joy. That means don't be afraid to make a bag or accessory for yourself!

I am constantly reminded of how fortunate I am. To be able to come up with creative ideas and spend time working on these handmade bags with friends is a blessing. To have the opportunity to make this book and share it with everyone is lucky. I am grateful also for the support that I have received from the growing number of people following my projects online. When I am happy, I look forward to making these handmade crafts, and when I am unhappy, I can turn to these projects to take my mind off of my worries. To be blessed is to be able to share your interests with others. This feeling of self-happiness is crucial in life, and I hope that I can always share this feeling.

Cherie Lee

Part 1: Bags, Pouches, and Purses

- Camera Bag
- Coin Purse
- Drawstring Bag
- Multi-Purpose Pouch
- Pencil Case
- Toiletries Bag
- Roomy Tote Bag

Whether you are taking a trip, visiting the corner store, attending a class, or just taking a walk, there is a useful bag here for you: a camera bag to protect your gadget when you go out to snap photos, a convenient drawstring bag for everyday use, a toiletries case to organize all your bottles... and more! The styles are gorgeous and the structures are super-functional. Make your next essential bag, pouch, or purse!

Camera Bag

Instructions p. 46

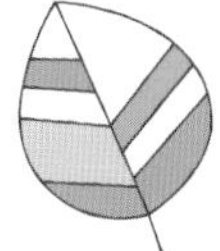

Camera Bag

Exploring new places with photography allows us to record the most unexpected moments and landscapes. This may be the purity of blue sky or green grass, surprising flowers on of the side of the road, children running excitedly down the street, or even a simple smile on a passerby's face. Sometimes there are no words to express the beauty that can be captured in a single photo. So protect your camera—your doorway to new expressions—with this portable case, and ensure you'll be able to take memorable photos for years to come.

Coin Purse

Instructions p. 49

Coin Purse

Sometimes it is the little things that make you feel good after a long day of work or class... like when you have just enough time to pop into a convenience store and pick out a tasty drink or snack to fuel your brain. Bring this small coin purse with you and you'll always have spare change on hand to grab that yummy bite to eat or leave the perfect tip.

Drawstring Bag

This drawstring bag is roomy and convenient, with enough space to put whatever it is you need to toss in before you leave. Easy to wash and super durable, this bag also makes a great gift for someone always on the go.

Drawstring Bag

Instructions p. 51

Multi-Purpose Pouch

Instructions p. 54

Multi-Purpose Pouch

When you leave your house, do you ever get that nagging feeling of "Did I remember my keys?" Do you find yourself rummaging through your purse every time that you need to find your keys? This pouch can help make sure you know exactly where those keys are when you need them. It can also be used to tote flash drives or other small, important items that tend to get lost in the shuffle.

Pencil Case

Instructions p. 56

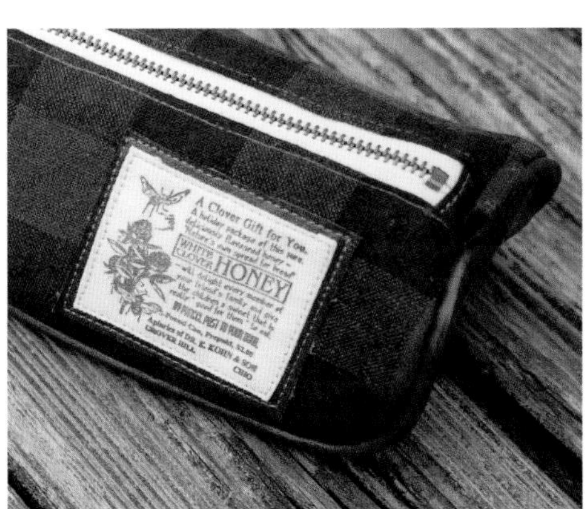

Pencil Case

You'll love this pencil case that you can take everywhere and pack with all the pens, pencils, highlighters, and erasers that you need. It's simple and soft, but sturdy, so it's sure to become a faithful companion.

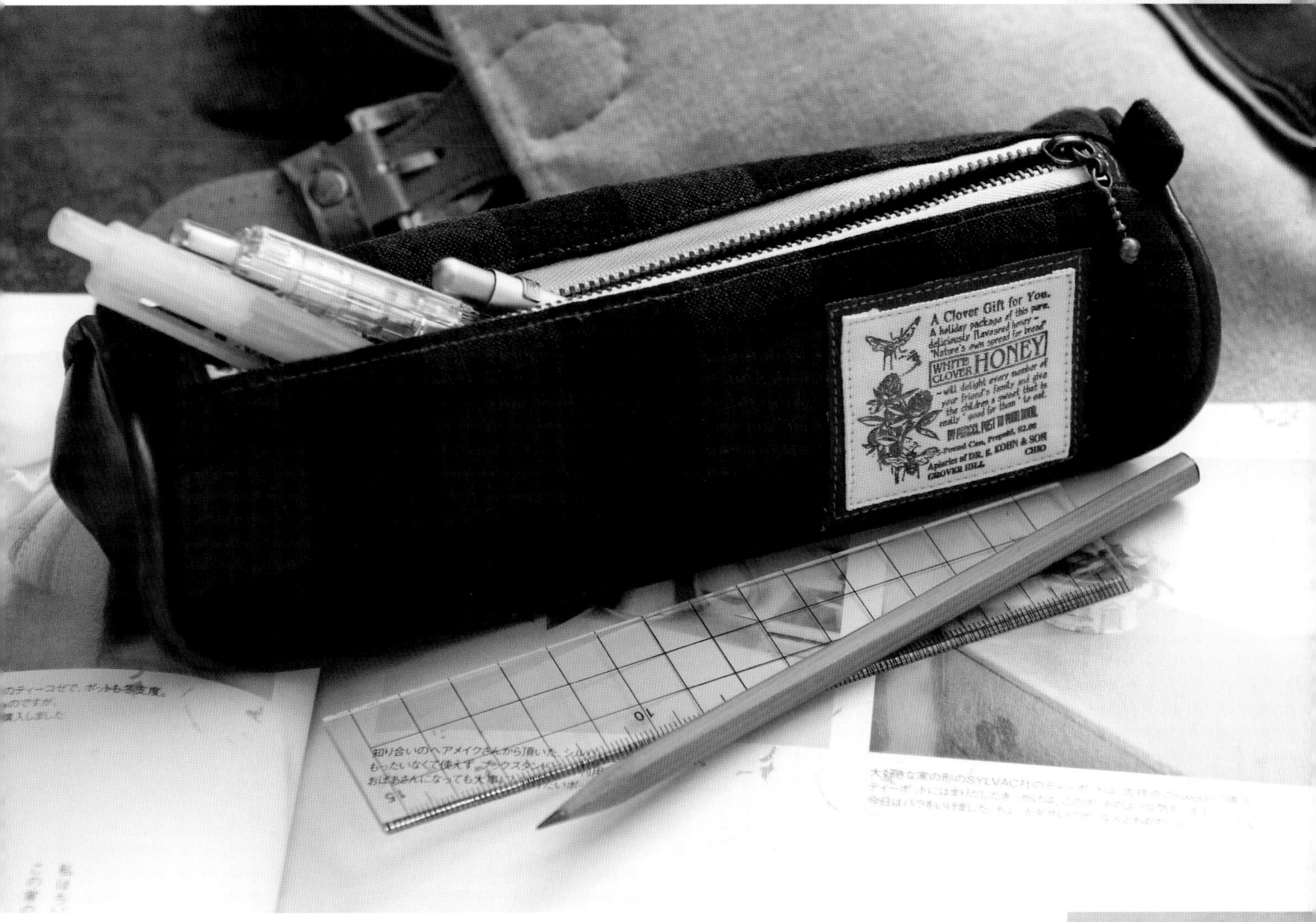

Toiletries Bag

Instructions p. 58

Toiletries Bag

Whether traveling for a night, a weekend, or weeks, you always need to take the time to gather your essential hygiene products, and it is important to have a bag to carry them in. This toiletries bag, with its sturdy frame and elastic pockets, will not only help to keep all of your products organized and tidy during your travels, but it will also make finding what you need convenient and quick.

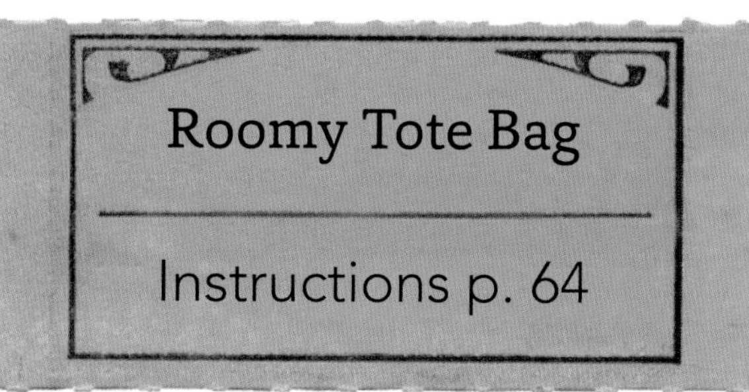
Roomy Tote Bag
Instructions p. 64

Roomy Tote Bag

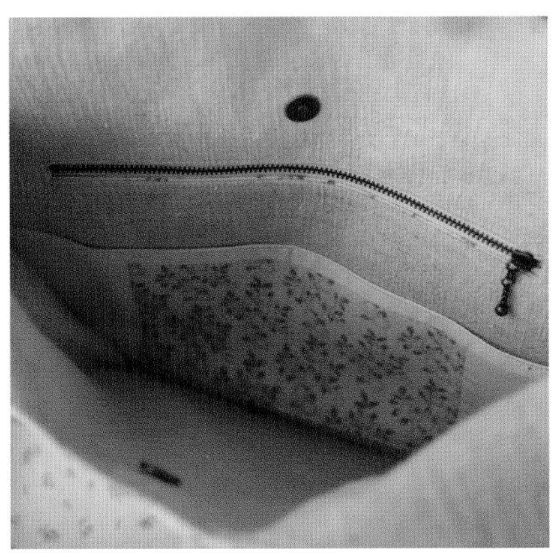

Sometimes you just have to carry a lot of stuff! This tote bag has all of the pockets and compartments you'll need to store everything for your outing, whether you are a mom carrying baby supplies, a shopper on a mission, or an athlete headed off to the gym. The inner zipper pocket is convenient for essentials such as a wallet, phone or keys.

Part 2: *Cases and Covers*

- Book Cover
- Cell Phone Sleeve
- Mini Binder
- Passport Case
- Notebook Cover
- Card Case
- Keepsake Folio

From book, notebook, and binder covers, to cases for business cards, passports, cell phones, and more, the projects in this section will protect your most valued and useful items, allow them to be conveniently at hand when you need them, and add a dash of style to your look to boot!

Book Cover

Instructions p. 70

Book Cover

You never know when you may be stuck waiting around for a bus or just have some time to kill, so it is nice to take a book on the road with you. But when we throw books in our purses, they always seem to end up getting banged and beat up. A cloth book cover is the perfect solution! Plus, if you don't want your neighbors on the bus to see what you are reading, this cover will keep your secret safe.

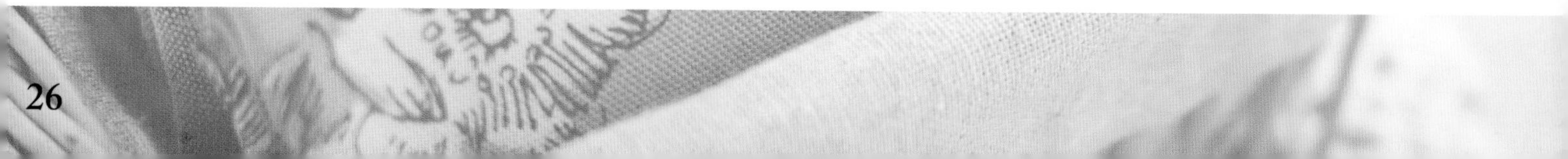

Cell Phone Sleeve

Instructions p. 73

Cell Phone Sleeve

This cell phone case is easy to make, lightweight, and incredibly useful. Avoid using magnetic buttons, which may interfere with your phone. Stick to little buttons to keep it stylish and convenient—just one little click, and you are looking right at your screen.

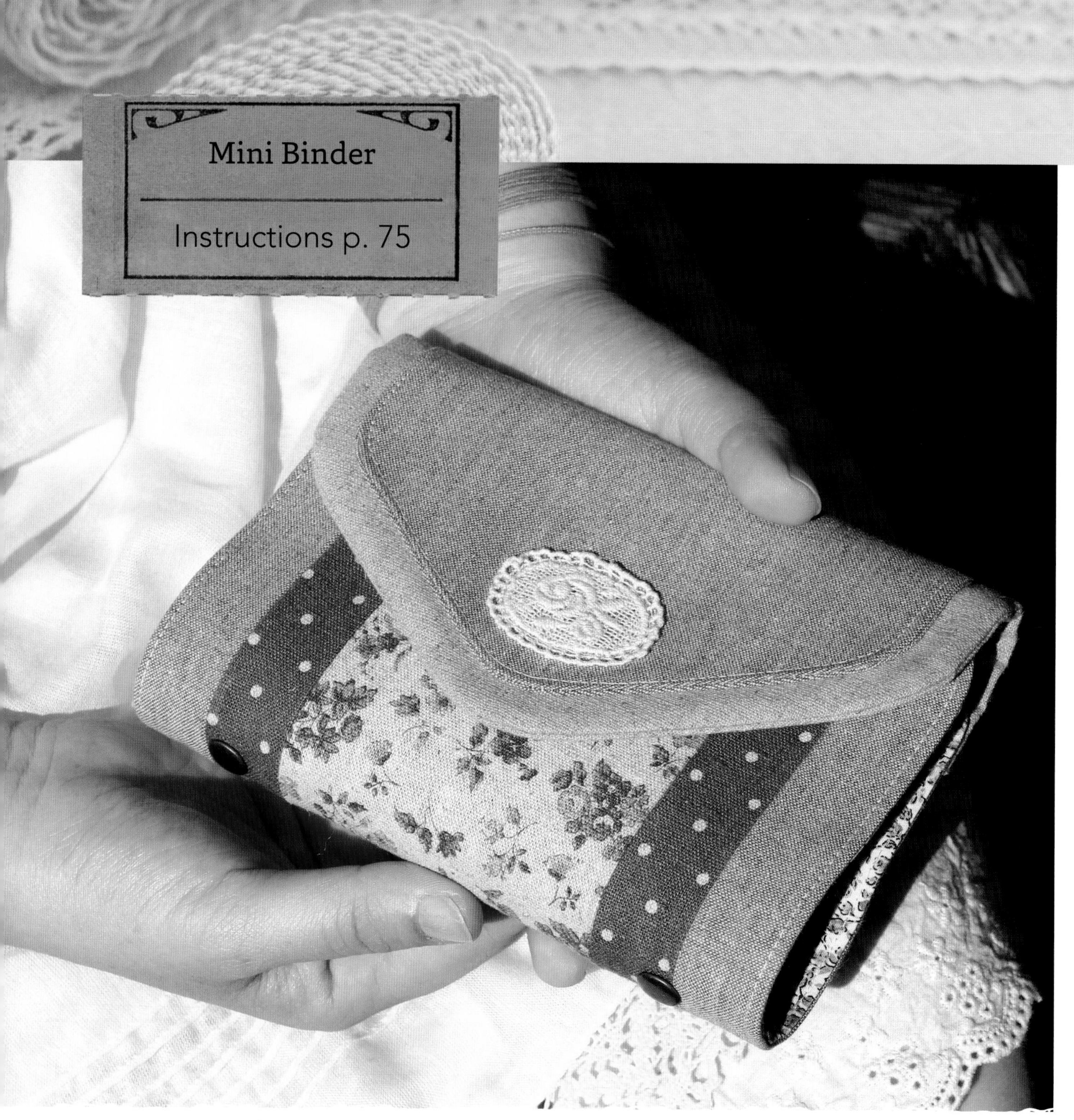

Mini Binder

We always search for that perfect binder to best suit our style and needs. Why have we never realized that the perfect one is the one we make ourselves? Your own handmade cloth binder will always be the best match for you, and it's much softer and cuter than hardback binders.

Passport Case

Instructions p. 78

Passport Case

The moment when you pull out your passport is an exciting moment of realization that you are about embark on a new journey. You're on your way to breathing foreign air, seeing new landscapes, tasting exotic foods, and admiring different cultures. Make sure you get to do all this stress-free by protecting the very thing that gets you there!

Notebook Cover

Instructions p. 81

Whether for work or for class, notebooks are crucial. This notebook cover can hold up to three notebooks at one time, and allows you to easily and quickly switch notebooks before class. There are also a few bonus pockets for you to slide in your pens and pencils, nice and secure.

Notebook Cover

Card Case

Instructions p. 84

Card Case

How do we end up with so many different types of cards? Membership cards, gift cards, VIP cards, credit cards, debit cards... Make this new home for your cards, and it's a guarantee that you will love how convenient all your cards are. You'll be able to easily and quickly find any card that you are looking for.

Keepsake Folio

Instructions p. 86

A small memory book can be a great present to give someone about to embark on travels, a mother with a new bundle of joy, or simply a friend ringing in the new year. This unique folio has a transparent pocket for important pictures, pockets to store special cards or documents, a handy pencil holder, and a place for a small notebook so that you can record exciting and important thoughts and events.

Keepsake Folio

Part 3: Accessories

- Slippers and Slipper Bag
- Water Bottle Sleeve
- Towel Clip
- Bucket Hat
- Baby's Bib

The assortment of accessories in this final section varies greatly, with items for use at all stages of life and all times of day—from bibs to slippers! You're sure to find these projects fun, cute, and, of course, totally functional. So whether you want to pop on your new bucket hat or go for a run with your new water bottle sleeve, enjoy the process of sewing these accessories.

Slippers and Slipper Bag

Instructions p. 92

Slippers and Slipper Bag

These handmade slippers offer the perfect level of comfort because you make them yourself. Homemade cozy footwear truly lets you lounge in comfort. Plus, sew a carry bag to take them with you on any trip to make the long, tiring journey more bearable.

Water Bottle Sleeve

Instructions p. 96

When going out, whether for a whole day or only for a few hours, you need to stay hydrated, so it is important to bring a water bottle or buy a beverage. But holding a drink is not convenient, and your things might get wet if you put it in your purse or bag. This water bottle sleeve is just the solution you're looking for!

Towel Clip

Towel Clip

Instructions p. 98

This cute bear clip is not only adorable, but will also come in handy for any mom. One side clips to your baby's towel or blanket, while the other side can clip onto clothes or a bag, making sure that your essential little towel doesn't slip away while you aren't looking.

Bucket Hat

Instructions p. 100

Bucket Hat

It is a wonderful feeling to be outside on a beautiful sunny day, but that sun can quickly become unbearable. This is why it is important to stay hydrated and spend time in the shade. This bucket hat will protect your head from sunburn, keep you cool, and shade your eyes.

Baby's Bib

Instructions p. 102

A mom can never have enough baby bibs, so these will always make great gifts! With super simple construction and utterly adorable designs, you can whip one of these bibs up in one sitting.

Baby's Bib

Instructions

Camera Bag

The finished camera bag measures 4¾" x 3" x 1⅛" (12 x 7.5 x 3cm).

Materials:

- ¼ yd. (¼m) of medium-weight fabric for main bag
- ⅛ yd. (⅛m) of complementing medium-weight fabric for contrast panel
- ¼ yd. (¼m) of lightweight fabric for lining
- ¼ yd. (¼m) of fusible fleece interfacing
- 6" (15cm) zipper
- 6" (15cm) of narrow decorative lace
- Small decorative lace medallion
- ⅜" (1cm) D-ring
- ⅜" (1cm) lobster clasp
- 1 yd. (1m) of ⅝" (1.6cm) wide bias binding tape or similar seam binding notion

Before you begin:

- Use a ⅜" (1cm) seam allowance unless indicated otherwise.
- Find and trace the 2 pattern pieces from Side B of the pattern paper, remembering to add ⅜" (1cm) seam allowances.
- You can iron extra layers of fusible fleece for the outer fabric and lining in order to provide more protection for your camera.

Cut the following pieces from your fabric and interfacing:

Note that the interfacing is cut without seam allowances to reduce bulk.

- **Bag Body** (from pattern pack): Main outer fabric (2), Lining fabric (2), Fusible fleece interfacing (4)
- **Contrast Panel** (from pattern pack): Contrast fabric (1)
- **Zipper Panels** – cut a 6½" x 1⅛" (16.5 x 3cm) rectangle: Main outer fabric (2), Lining fabric (2), Fusible fleece interfacing (2)
- **Bag Sides** – cut a 10⅝" x 2" (27 x 5cm) rectangle: Main outer fabric (1), Lining fabric (1), Fusible fleece interfacing (1)
- **Strap** – cut a 24⅜" x 1⅜" (62 x 3.5cm) rectangle: Main outer fabric (1)
- **Inner Pocket** – cut a 4¾" x 3⅛" (12 x 8cm) rectangle: Main outer fabric (2)
- **D-Ring Loop** – cut a 3½" x 1⅜" (9 x 3.5cm) rectangle: Main outer fabric (1)

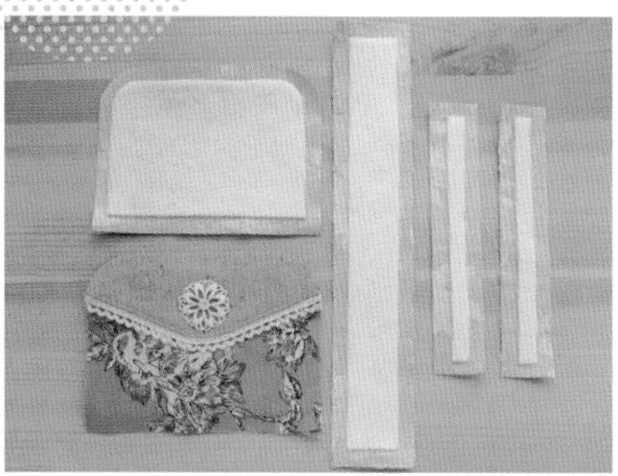

01. Refer to steps 4 and 5 of the Book Cover (pg. 71) to see how to apply the contrast panel to the bag body outer fabric. Iron the fusible fleece interfacing to the corresponding outer fabrics (note that it is without seam allowances).

02. Iron the fusible fleece interfacing to the corresponding lining fabrics as well. Apply the inner pocket to one of the bag body lining pieces; See Essential Techniques C: Version 2 (pg. 111) for instructions on this.

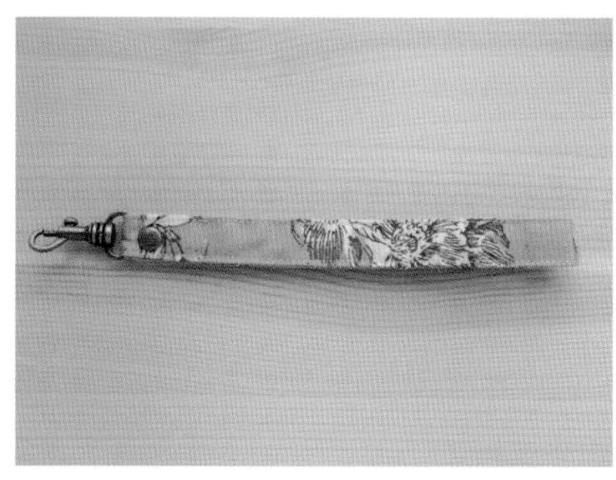

03. Using a ¾" (1.8cm) bias tape maker, make a strap from the strap fabric. Refer to Essential Techniques H (pg. 119) for further instructions on this.

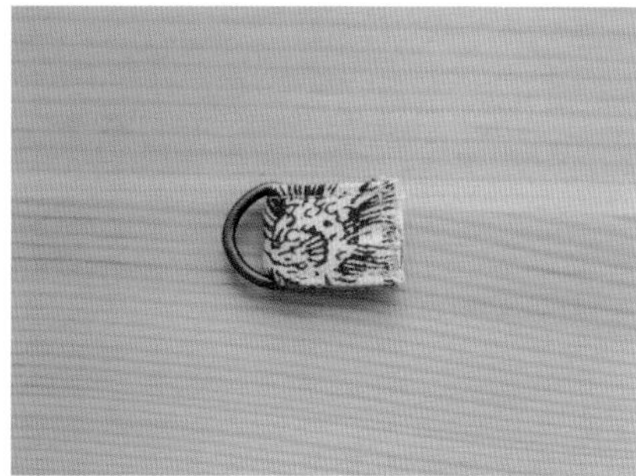

04. For the D-ring loop, fold under the long edges toward the center of the strip, then fold the entire strip in half lengthwise with wrong sides together. Edge stitch down both long edges of the strip, then loop it through the D-ring and baste its ends in place.

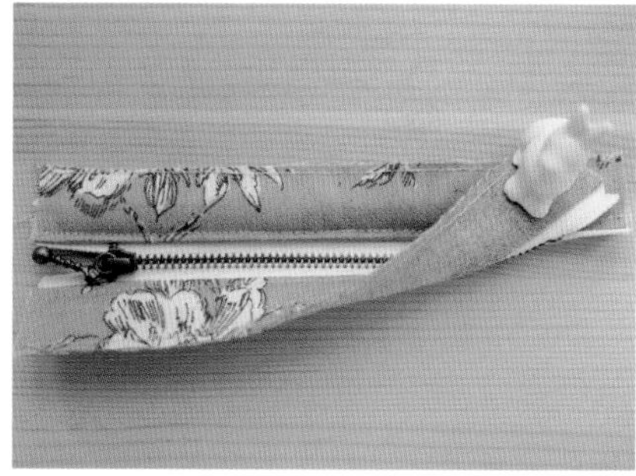

05. Layer the zipper tape between the long edges of the outer fabric and lining zipper panels with right sides facing. Sew the three layers together and press the fabric away from the zipper. Repeat with the remaining zipper panels and the other side of the zipper tape.

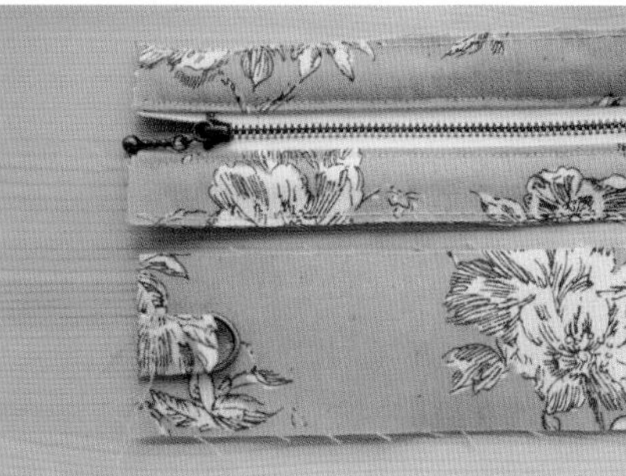

06. Line up the D-ring loop along the short edge of the bag side. With the D-ring pointing inward, baste it in place.

07. Layer one of the short ends of the zipper panel between the short ends of the bag side lining and outer fabric with right sides together. Sew the layers together along this edge.

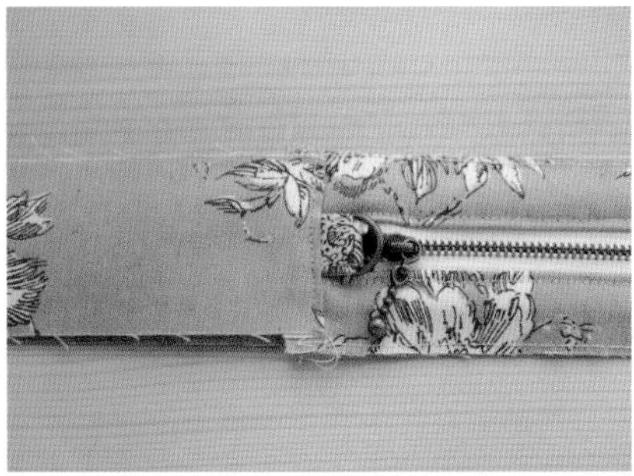

08. Flip the fabric out so the right sides are facing outward and edge stitch the seam.

09. Repeat steps 7 and 8 with the remaining end of the zipper tape and bag sides. When you finish you should have a ring.

10. Layer the bag body lining and outer fabric together with wrong sides facing. Baste around the entire edge of the fabrics. Repeat this with the remaining two bag body lining and outer fabric pieces.

11. Line up the bottom center of the bag side with the bottom center of the bag body. Sew the fabrics together along this bottom edge, but stop short ⅜" (1cm) of each corner.

12. Match up the remaining raw edges along the side and top of the bag body and sides, making a sharp 90 degree turn at the bottom corners.

13. Trim the seam allowance to ¼" (0.5cm) and, using the bias tape, bind the raw edges of the seam. Repeat steps 11–13 for the other side of the bag.

14. You have now completed your portable camera bag.

Coin Purse

The finished coin purse measures 5⅜" x 3½" (13.5 x 9cm).

Materials:

- ⅛ yd. (⅛m) of medium to heavyweight fabric for main purse
- ⅛ yd. (⅛m) of complementing medium to heavyweight fabric for piping
- ⅛ yd. (⅛m) of lightweight fabric for lining
- ⅛ yd. (⅛m) of heavyweight interfacing
- 4" (10cm) zipper
- 10" (25cm) of cording for piping
- 13" (33cm) of ⅝" wide bias tape or similar seam binding notion
- Small decorative cloth patch

Before you begin:

- Use a ⅜" (1cm) seam allowance unless indicated otherwise.
- Find and trace the 1 pattern piece from Side B of the pattern paper, remembering to add ⅜" (1cm) seam allowances.

Cut the following pieces from your fabric:

- **Purse Body** (from pattern pack): Main outer fabric (2), Lining fabric (2), Heavyweight interfacing (2)
- **Piping** – cut an 11" x 1⅛" (28 x 3cm) rectangle: Contrast fabric (1)
- **Zipper Tabs** – cut a 1½" x 2⅜" (4 x 6cm) rectangle: Contrast fabric (2)

Instructions

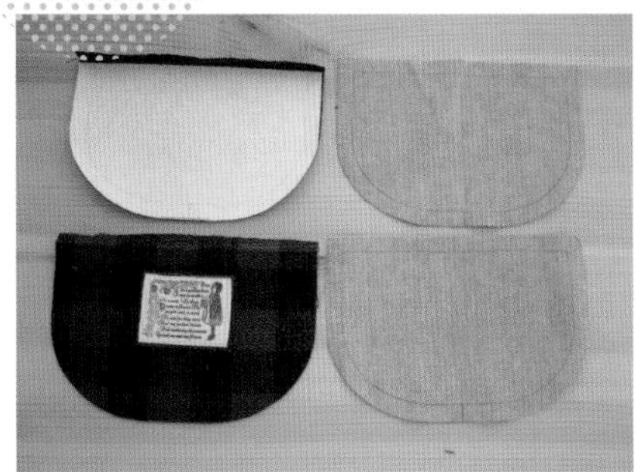

01. Iron the interfacing to the outer fabrics, then apply the cotton patch to what will be the front of the coin purse.

02. For the zipper tabs, fold under the short edges by ⅜" (1cm). Then fold the entire tab in half with wrong sides facing, bringing together the folds. Wrap those folds over the ends of the zipper, then edge stitch them in place.

03. Layer the zipper tape between the top edges of the outer purse fabric and lining. Match up the edges, then sew the three layers together.

04. Repeat this for the other side of the zipper tape and the remaining outer purse and lining pieces.

05. Take the piping fabric and fold under the short ends by ⅜" (1cm). Line it up along the bottom curved edge of the outer purse fabric, between the pattern markings, and baste it in place.

06. Lay a piece of cording inside the piping fabric and fold the other long edge of the piping over it.

07. Baste the fold in place close to the cording.

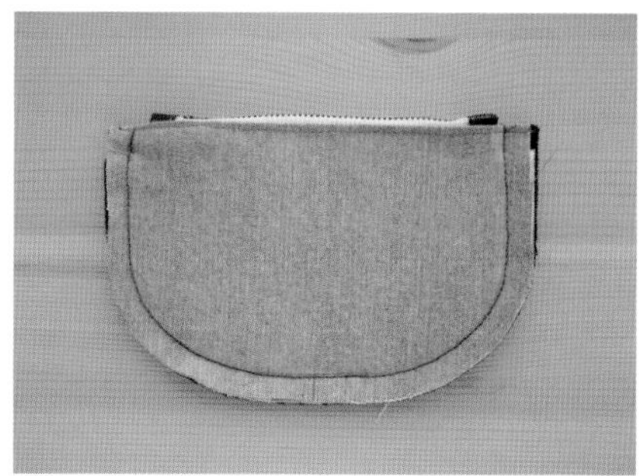

08. Layer the fabrics over one another with outer fabrics facing each other inward and lining fabrics facing outward. Sew the layers together along the curved edge.

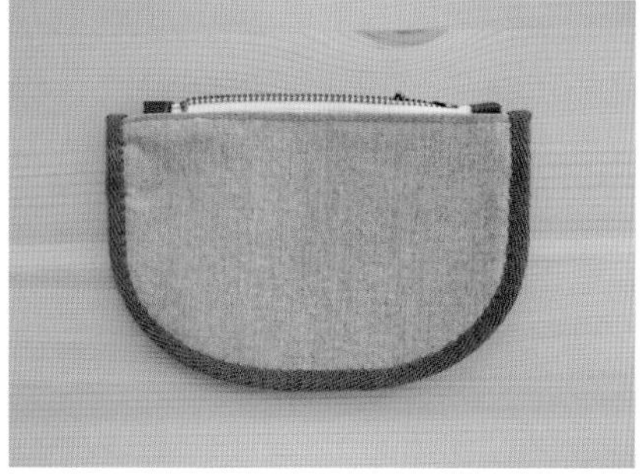

09. Trim the seam allowance to ¼" (0.5cm) and bind the raw edges of the previous seam with ⅝" (1.6cm) wide bias tape.

10. The small coin purse is now complete.

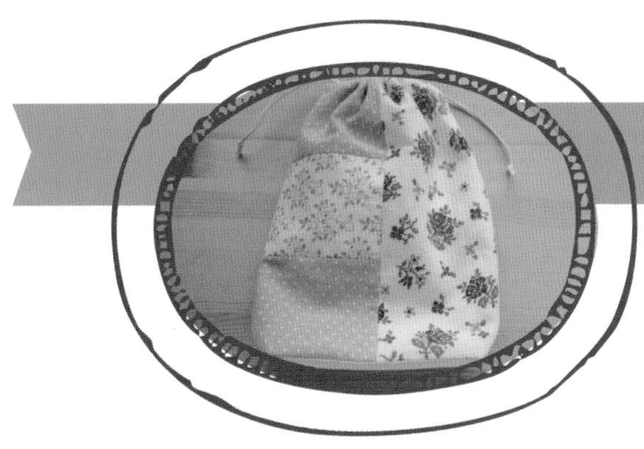

Drawstring Bag

The finished large bag measures 11⅞" x 11" x 3⅛" (30 x 28 x 8cm), while the small bag measures 8⅝" x 11" x 3⅛" (22 x 28 x 8cm).

Materials:

FOR LARGE BAG:

- ⅓ yd. (⅓m) of light to medium-weight fabric for back and front – Fabric A
- ¼ yd. (¼m) of light to medium-weight fabric for sides – Fabric B
- ⅓ yd. (⅓m) of lightweight fabric for lining
- ⅛ yd. (⅛m) of complementing light to medium-weight fabric for drawstring casings
- 55⅛" (140cm) of cording for drawstring

FOR SMALL BAG:

- ⅓ yd. (⅓m) of light to medium-weight fabric for front – Fabric A
- ¼ yd. (¼m) of light to medium-weight fabric for back panels – Fabric B
- ¼ yd. (¼m) of light to medium-weight fabric for center back – Fabric C
- ⅓ yd. (⅓m) of lightweight fabric for lining
- ⅛ yd. (⅛m) of complementing light to medium-weight fabric for drawstring casings
- 39⅜" (100cm) of cording for drawstring

Before you begin:

- Use a ⅜" (1cm) seam allowance unless indicated otherwise.
- This bag is made without interfacing to be more soft and flexible.

Cut the following pieces from your fabric:

- **Large Tote Bag:**
  - Bag Front and Back – cut a 9½" x 11⅞" (24 x 30cm) rectangle: Fabric A (2), Lining fabric (2)
  - Bag Sides – cut a 4" x 11⅞" (10 x 30cm) rectangle: Fabric B (2), Lining fabric (2)
  - Bag Bottom – cut a 4" x 9½" (10 x 24cm) rectangle: Fabric A (1), Lining fabric (1)
  - Drawstring Casings – cut an 11⅞" x 1½" (30 x 4cm) rectangle: Contrast fabric (2)
- **Small Tote Bag:**
  - Bag Front – Constructed as patchwork:
    - Piece B – cut a 9½" x 4¾" (24 x 12cm) rectangle: Fabric B (1)
    - Piece C – cut a 9½" x 4⅜" (24 x 11cm) rectangle: Fabric C (1)
    - Piece D – cut a 9½" x 4⅜" (24 x 11cm) rectangle: Fabric B (1)
  - Bag Back – cut a 9½" x 11⅞" (24 x 30cm) rectangle: Fabric A (1), Lining fabric (2)
  - Bag Bottom – cut a 7" x 3⅛" (18 x 8cm) rectangle: Fabric A (1), Lining fabric (1)
  - Drawstring Casings – cut an 8⅝" x 1½" (22 x 4cm) rectangle: Contrast fabric (2)

Instructions

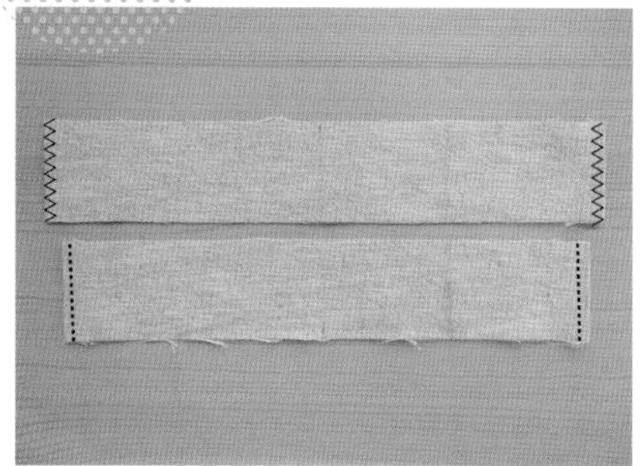

01. For the large bag, sew a zigzag seam on the short edges of the drawstring casing pieces, along the raw edges. Then fold under the zigzagged edges by ⅜" (1cm) and edge stitch the fold in place.

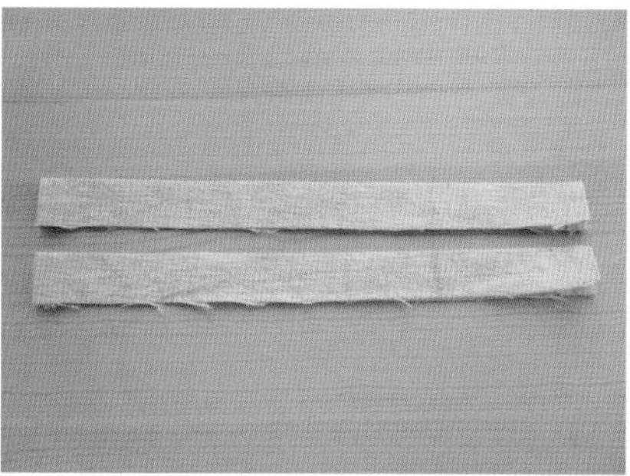

02. Fold the pieces lengthwise with wrong sides together and baste the raw edges to secure them.

03. Line up the bag front and back to the bag sides along the 11⅞" (30cm) edges, alternating them, then joining them in a ring to create a square as seen in the photograph. Sew them together along the raw edges, being sure to stop ⅜" (1cm) before the bottom edge.

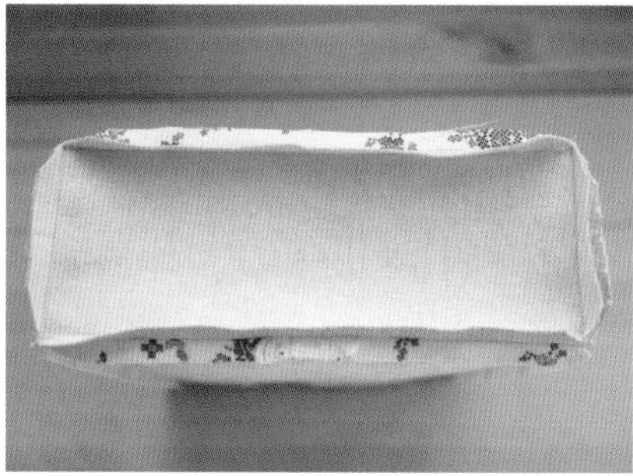

04. Sew the bag bottom around the bottom edge of the bag body. When complete, trim the four corners. Repeat steps 3 and 4 for the lining part of the bag as well.

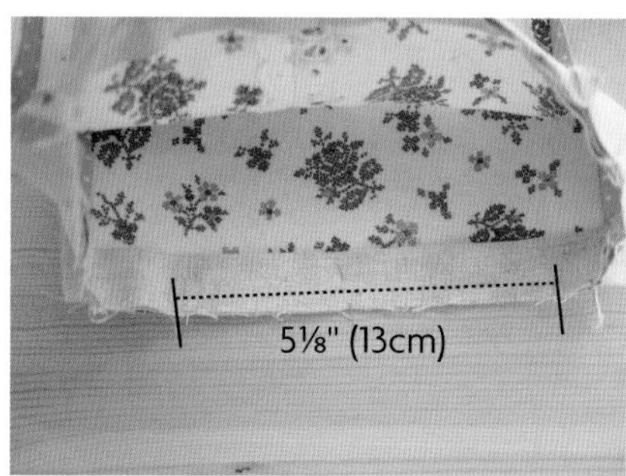

05. Take the drawstring casing from step 2 and line up the raw edge against the top edge of the bag front. Baste it in place along the raw edge. Repeat this on the bag back, but sew a 5⅛" (13cm) seam centered along the middle of the casing instead.

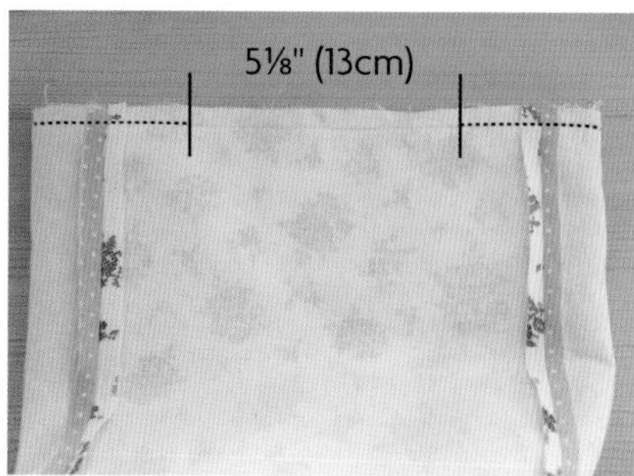

06. Put the bag lining into the outer bag with right sides together, lining up the top edges. Sew a seam around the perimeter of the bag, skipping over the 5⅛" (13cm) section already sewn in the previous step.

07. Turn the bag right side out from the opening in the top, then edge stitch around the top edge of the bag.

08. Thread the cording through the drawstring casing to finish the large tote bag.

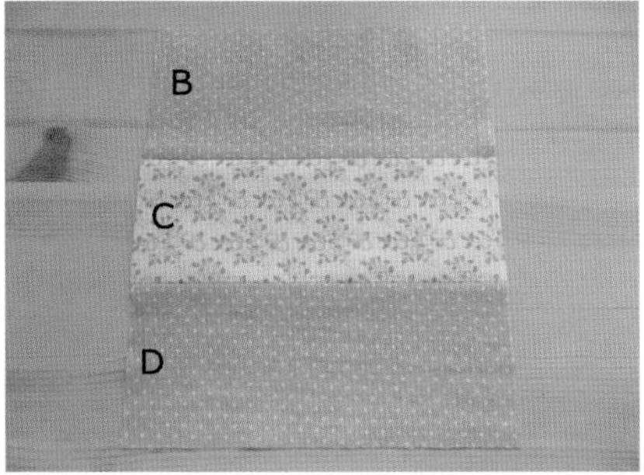

09. To make the small tote, sew together fabric pieces B, C, and D in a row along the 9½" (24cm) sides.

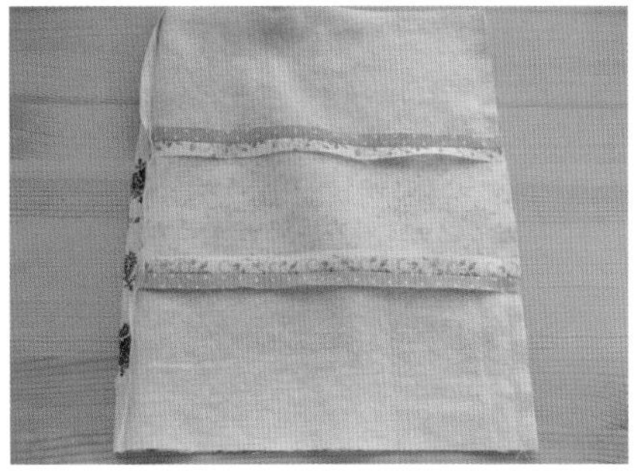

10. Position this piece over fabric A, matching up the side edges. Sew them together along the sides and iron the seams.

11. Follow steps 1 and 2 to create the drawstring casings for your bag. Sew them to the top edge of the bag as in step 5, but sew the second casing with a 3⅛" (8cm) long seam instead.

12. Line up the bag bottom around the bottom edge of the bag body and sew it in place. Clip the seam allowances at the corners.

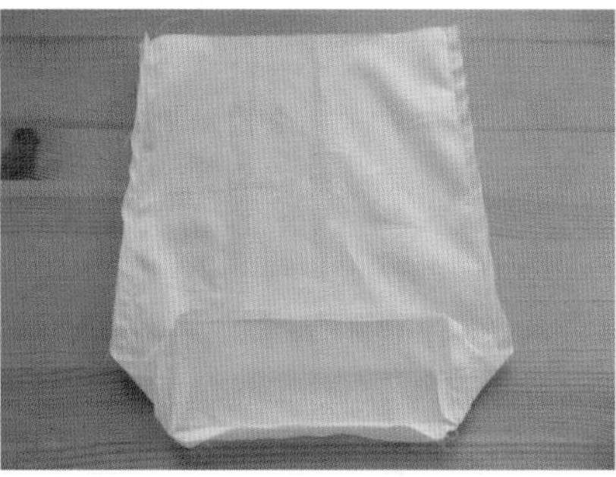

13. Repeat the same steps for the lining of the bag, sewing the bag front and back together along the sides, then sewing on the bag bottom as in the previous step.

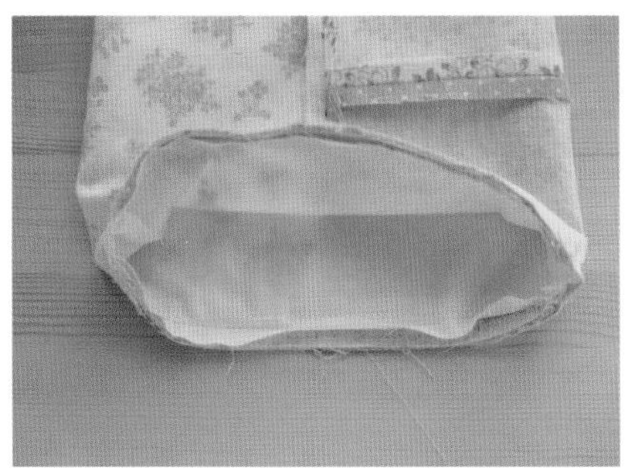

14. Put the bag lining into the outer bag and match up the raw edges, then sew around the perimeter of the top of the bag as in step 6, skipping over the stitching line sewn previously in step 11.

15. Turn the bag right side out from the opening in the top, then edge stitch around the top edge of the bag.

16. Thread the cording through the casing and you have finished your drawstring bag.

Multi-Purpose Pouch

The finished pouch measures 2½" x 4⅜" (6.5 x 11cm).

Materials:

- ⅛ yd. (⅛m) of light to medium-weight fabric for main pouch
- ⅛ yd. (⅛m) of complementing light to medium-weight fabric for contrast panel
- ⅛ yd. (⅛m) of lightweight fabric for lining
- ⅛ yd. (⅛m) of heavyweight interfacing
- Metal snap
- Metal latch clasps (as many as desired)
- Metal rivets (one for each latch clasp)
- 22" (56cm) of bias binding tape or fabric to make your own
- Small decorative lace medallion

Before you begin:

- Use a ⅜" (1cm) seam allowance unless indicated otherwise.
- Find and trace the 1 pattern piece from Side B of the pattern paper.

Cut the following pieces from your fabric:

- **Outer Pouch:**
  - Upper Panel – cut a 7½" x 3⅛" (19 x 8cm) rectangle: Main outer fabric (1)
  - Side Panel – cut a 7½" x 2" (19 x 5cm) rectangle: Contrast fabric (1)
- **Inner Pouch:**
  - Pouch Lining (from pattern pack): Lining fabric (1), Heavyweight interfacing (1)
  - Center Panel – cut a 3⅛" x 4⅜" (8 x 11cm) rectangle: Contrast fabric (1)

Instructions

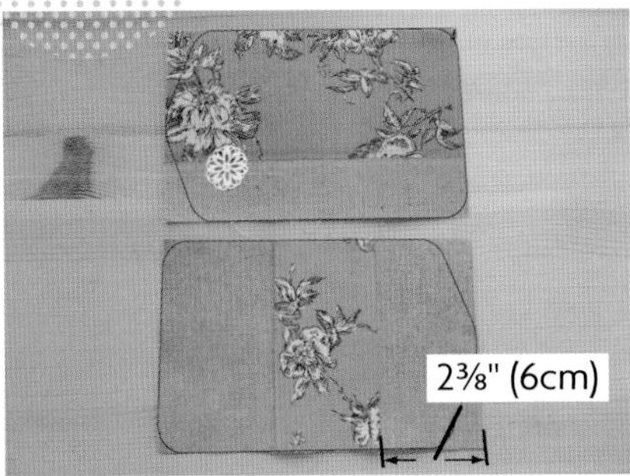

01. Line up the outer pouch fabrics together along the 7½" (19cm) edges. Sew them together, apply the lace medallion, and iron on the interfacing. For the inner pouch, fold under the 4⅜" (11cm) edges of the center panel by ⅜" (1cm) on each side, then edge stitch the folds in place on the pouch lining where the pattern indicates. Use the paper pattern to trim the fabric to the proper shape.

02. Layer the outer and lining fabric together with wrong sides facing, then baste the edges together.

03. Refer to Essential Techniques K (pg. 122) to apply bias binding around the perimeter of the pouch.

04. Once done with the binding, mark the placement of the metal snaps according to the pattern guidelines.

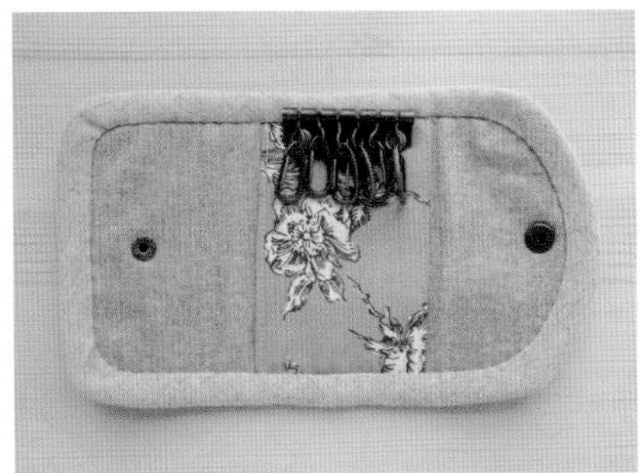

05. Install the metal snaps. Then, using metal rivets, attach the key holders to the top edge of the contrast inner center panel.

06. You now have a safe and easy place to store your keys or other valuables.

Pencil Case

The finished pencil bag measures 8¼" x 3⅛" x 2⅜" (21 x 8 x 6cm).

Materials:

- ⅛ yd. (⅛m) of medium-weight fabric for main bag
- ⅛ yd. (⅛m) of complementing medium-weight fabric for bag bottom and piping
- ⅛ yd. (⅛m) of lightweight fabric for lining
- 7" (18cm) zipper
- Small decorative cloth patch
- 30" (76cm) of ⅝" (1.6cm) wide bias binding tape or similar seam binding notion
- 30" (76cm) of thin cording for piping

Before you begin:

- Use a ⅜" (1cm) seam allowance unless indicated otherwise.
- Find and trace the 2 pattern pieces from Side B of the pattern paper, remembering to add ⅜" (1cm) seam allowances.

Cut the following pieces from your fabric:

- **Case Sides** (from pattern pack): Main outer fabric (2), Lining fabric (2)
- **Case Bottom** (from pattern pack): Contrast fabric (1), Lining fabric (1)
- **Piping** – cut a 28⅜" x 1⅛" (72 x 3cm) rectangle: Contrast fabric (1)
- **Zipper Tabs** – cut a 2⅜" x 1½" (6 x 4cm) rectangle: Contrast fabric (2)
- **End Tab** – cut a 4" x 1¾" (10 x 4.5cm) rectangle: Main outer fabric (1)

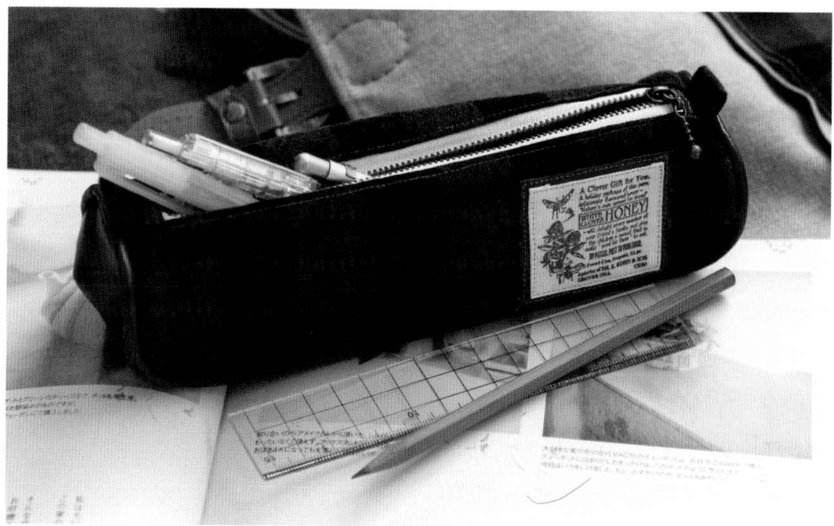

Instructions

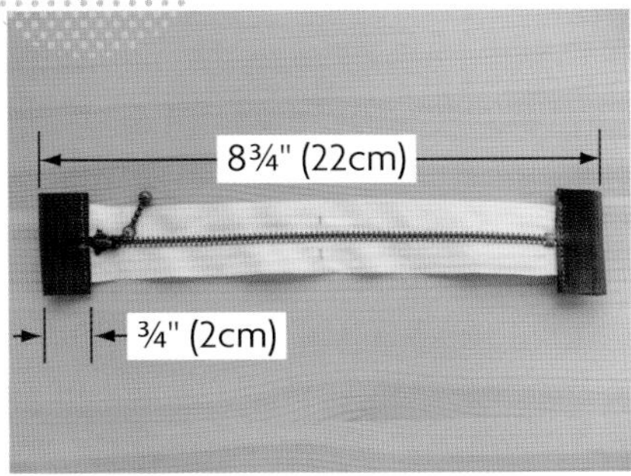

01. For the zipper tabs, fold under each short edge by ⅜" (1cm), then fold the entire tab in half, bringing the folds together with wrong sides facing. Wrap the tabs round the ends of the zipper and edge stitch the folds in place.

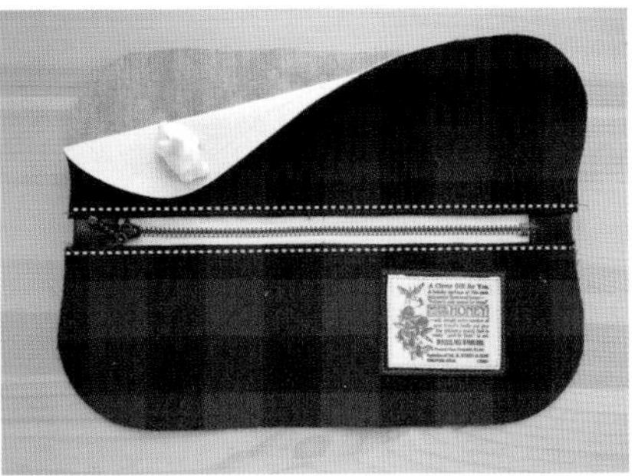

02. Sew the decorative patch to the corner of one of the bag sides. Layer the zipper tape between the long edges of the outer bag side and lining with right sides facing. Sew through the three layers, then edge stitch the previous seam. Repeat this with the remaining bag side fabric outer fabric and lining.

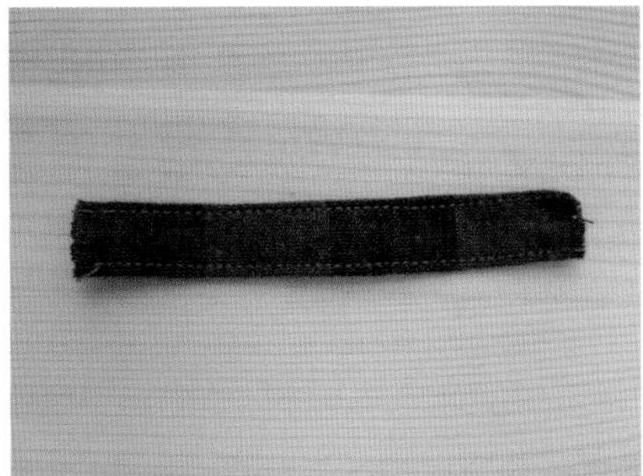

03. For the end tab, fold the strip in half lengthwise with right sides together. Sew it along the long edge with a ¼" (0.7cm) seam allowance and turn the tube right side out. Iron it flat, then edge stitch it along both edges.

04. Cut the strip in half, then fold the halves in half and line up the raw edges along the ends of the zipper. Baste them in place along the zipper tabs from step 1.

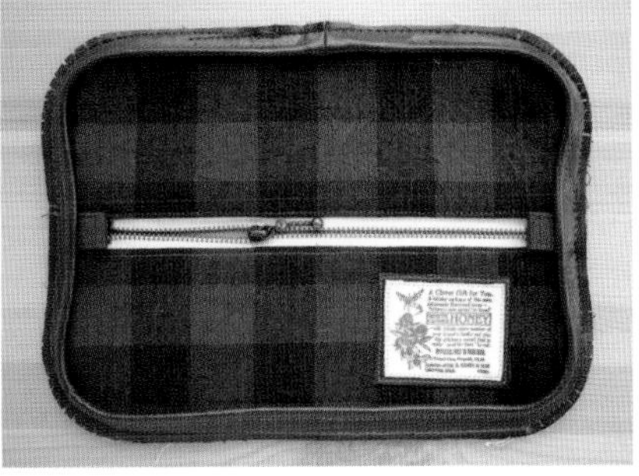

05. Refer to Essential Techniques K (pg. 122) and use the piping fabric and cording to attach piping around the borders of the bag sides.

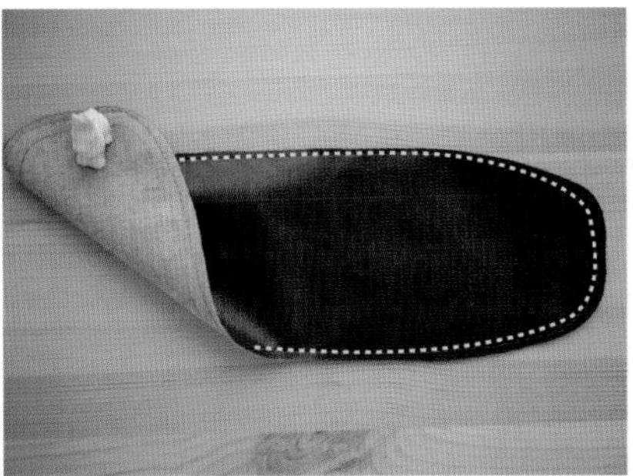

06. Line up the bag bottom outer fabric and lining with wrong sides together and baste them together around the raw edges.

07. Line up the perimeter of the bag bottom with the edges of the bag sides and sew the edges together.

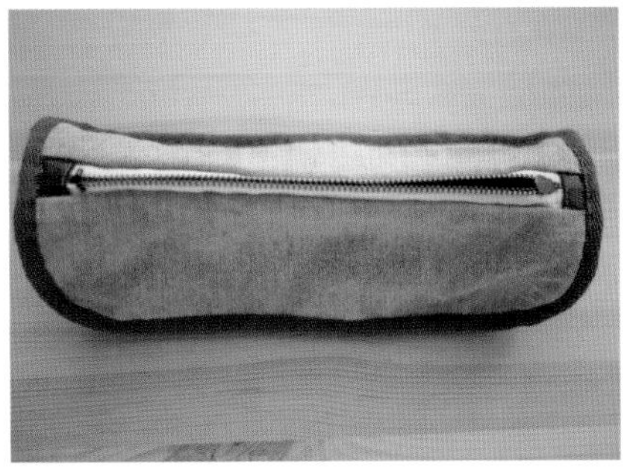

08. Trim the seam allowance to ¼" (0.5cm) and use the bias tape to bind the previous seam.

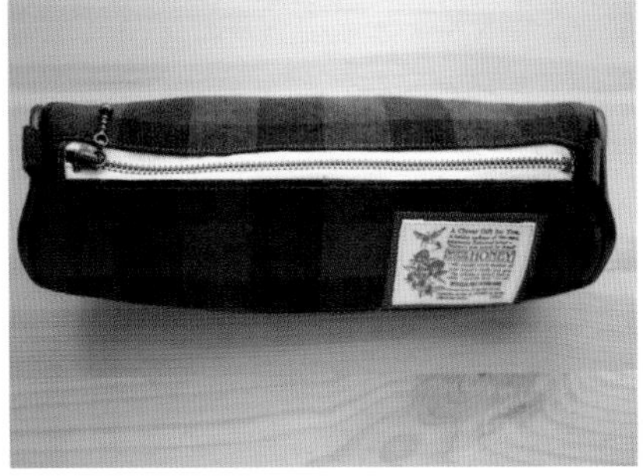

09. You have now finished your pencil case.

Toiletries Bag

The finished bag measures 8¼" x 5⅞" x 5⅛" (21 x 15 x 13cm).

Materials:

- ¼ yd. (¼m) of medium-weight fabric for main bag
- ¼ yd. (¼m) of complementing medium-weight fabric for bottom and back of bag
- ⅔ yd. (⅔m) of lightweight fabric for lining
- ⅔ yd. (⅔m) of 44" (112cm) wide or 1¼ yds. (1¼m) of 22" (56cm) wide heavyweight interfacing
- 22" (56cm) zipper
- 7" (18cm) zipper
- 23" (58cm) of ¼" (0.8cm) wide elastic
- 23" (58cm) of wide decorative lace
- Two metal rivets
- Leather strap for handle
- Small decorative metal medallion

Before you begin:

- Use a ⅜" (1cm) seam allowance unless indicated otherwise.
- Find and trace the 1 pattern piece from Side A of the pattern paper, remembering to add ⅜" (1cm) seam allowances.

Cut the following pieces from your fabric and interfacing:

- **Top Zipper Pocket:**
  - Upper Zipper Pocket – cut a 9" x 2" (23 x 5cm) rectangle: Lining fabric (2), Heavyweight interfacing (1)
  - Lower Zipper Pocket – cut a 9" x 4⅜" (23 x 11cm) rectangle: Lining fabric (2), Heavyweight interfacing (1)
  - Zipper Tabs – cut a 2¾" x 1⅛" (7 x 3cm) rectangle: Lining fabric (2)
- **Bag Top** (from pattern pack): Main outer fabric (1), Lining fabric (1), Heavyweight interfacing (3)
- **Bag Bottom** (from pattern pack): Contrast fabric (1), Lining fabric (1), Heavyweight interfacing (2)
- **Bag Body:**
  - Upper Bag Front – cut a 22⅞" x 2" (58 x 5cm) rectangle: Contrast fabric (1), Lining fabric (1), Heavyweight interfacing (2)
  - Lower Bag Front – cut a 22⅞" x 4⅜" (58 x 11cm) rectangle: Main outer fabric (1), Lining fabric (1), Heavyweight interfacing (2)
- **Bag Back** – cut a 5⅞" x 4⅜" (15 x 11cm) rectangle: Outer fabric (1), Lining fabric (1), Heavyweight interfacing (2)
- **Elastic Pocket** – cut a 28¾" x 4" (73 x 10cm) rectangle: Lining fabric (2), Heavyweight interfacing (1)

Follow the measurements below for the inner elastic pockets:

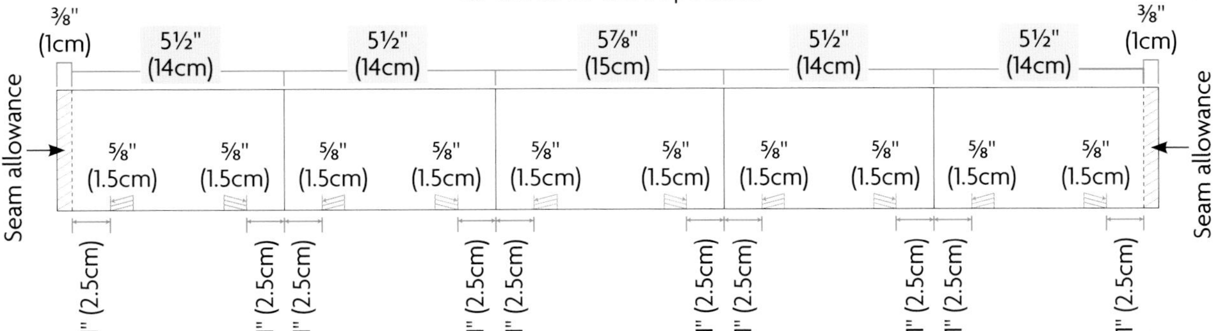

Instructions

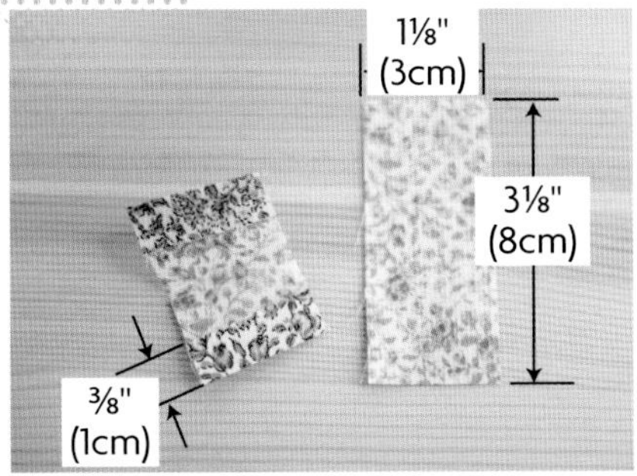

01. For the zipper pocket found inside the flap of the bag, first take the zipper tabs and fold under the short edges by ⅜" (1cm). Then fold the entire tab in half with wrong sides together and iron it flat.

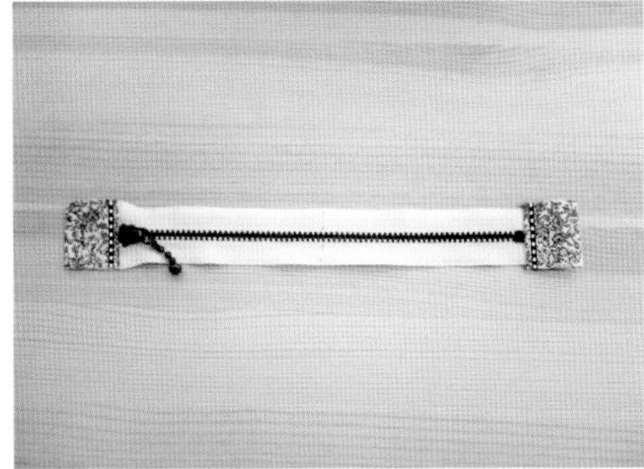

02. Fold the tabs around the ends of the 7" (18cm) zipper and edge stitch them in place along the folds.

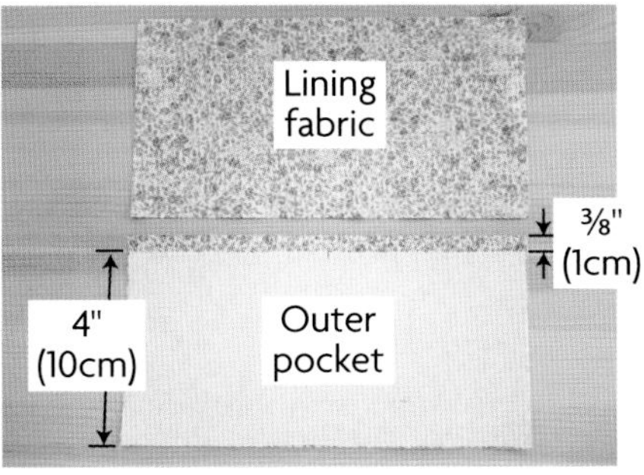

03. Take the lower zipper pocket interfacing and trim it to 9" x 4" (23 x 10cm). Iron it along the bottom edge of the corresponding main fabric. Take both pocket fabrics (the non-interfaced fabric will serve as lining) and fold under one long edge by ⅜" (1cm). Do not iron any interfacing to the lining, as this will create too much bulk.

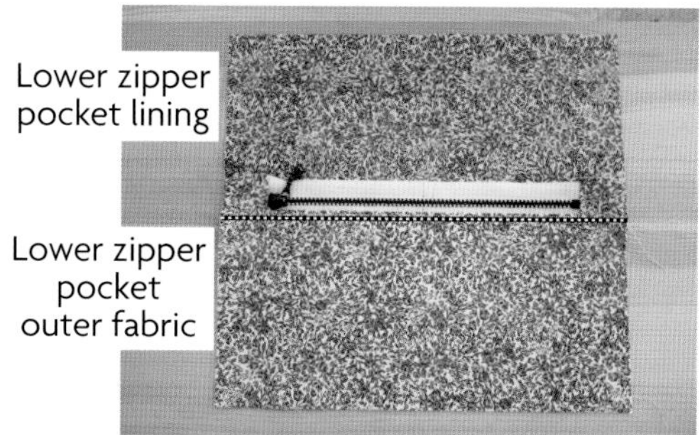

04. Use a strip of fusible web or fabric glue to fuse the folded edge of the outer lower zipper pocket to one edge of the zipper tape (right sides both facing up). Repeat this with the folded edge of the lining piece on the back side of the zipper. When this is complete, edge stitch the folds in place.

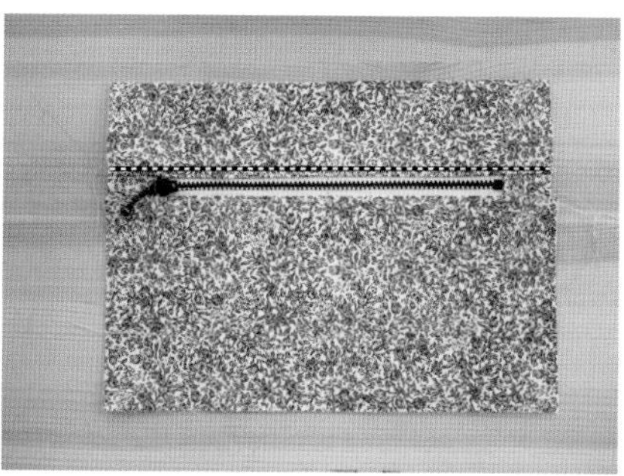

05. Repeat steps 3 and 4 with the upper zipper pocket pieces (trimming the interfacing to 9" x 1½" [23 x 4cm]). Fuse, then sew the folded edges along the other side of the zipper tape.

06. Iron the corresponding interfacing to one of the bag top lining pieces, then layer it beneath the zipper pocket just sewn in the previous step (right sides both facing up). Trim the zipper pocket fabric to make it the same shape as the lining, then baste the layers together.

07. The zipper pocket for the bag top is now finished.

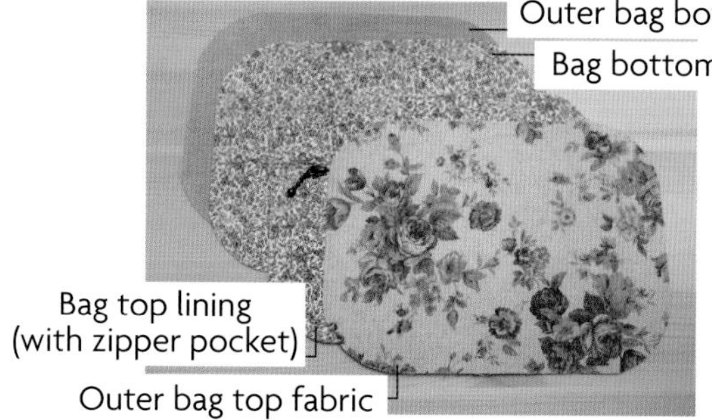

08. Take the rest of the bag top and bottom fabrics and iron on their respective interfacing pieces. For the outer bag top piece, iron an additional layer of interfacing with the seam allowances cut off for extra sturdiness.

09. To create the elastic pockets, fuse the interfacing (trimmed to 28¾" x 3⅛" [73 x 8cm]) to the back side of what will be the outer pocket. Layer the two pocket pieces together with right sides facing and sew them together along the top edge.

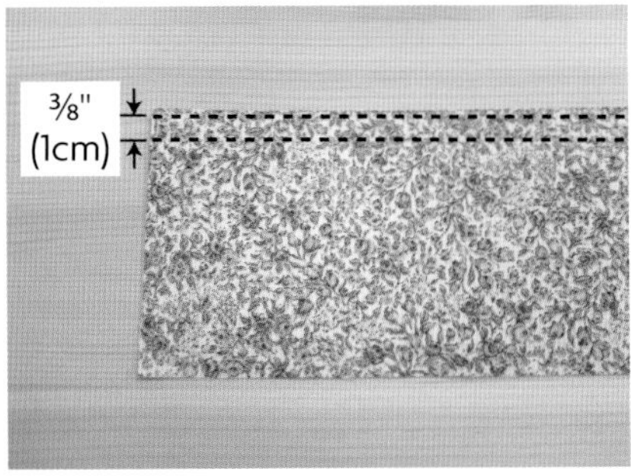

10. Turn the fabric right side out and top stitch two seams across the top, one 1⁄16" (0.2cm) from the edge and the other ½" (1.2cm) from the edge.

11. Following the illustration on page 59, create pleats along the bottom edge of the pocket fabric, holding the folds in place with pins.

12. Iron the interfacing to the lower bag front lining fabric, then line up the pleated edge of the pocket against the bottom edge of the lower bag front. Baste the pocket fabric in place along the entire bottom edge.

13. Use a bodkin to pull the elastic through the casing sewn in step 10.

14. Pull the elastic to the length that suits you and the strength of the material so it isn't stretched beyond its capacity. Once the correct length is within the casing, anchor both ends of the elastic to the fabric, then trim off any excess elastic. Baste the sides of the pocket fabric to the side edges of the lower bag front piece. Sew vertical seams throughout the pocket too, as the illustration on page 59 indicates.

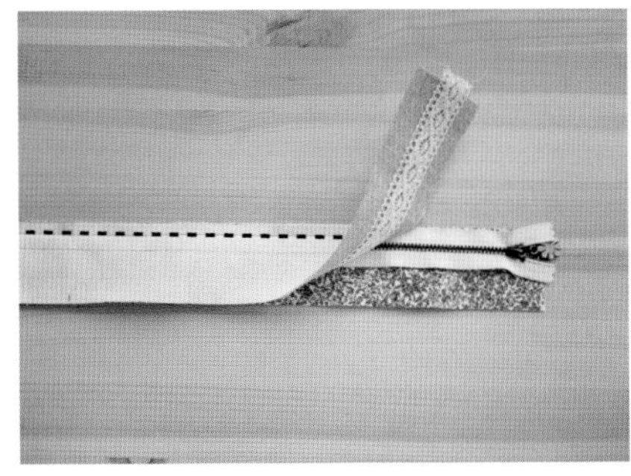

15. Iron the interfacing to the upper bag front outer and lining pieces. Sew the lace across the outer fabric. Layer the 22" (56cm) zipper between these outer and lining fabrics, matching up the long edges with the zipper tape. Sew the layers together with a 5⁄16" (0.7cm) seam allowance.

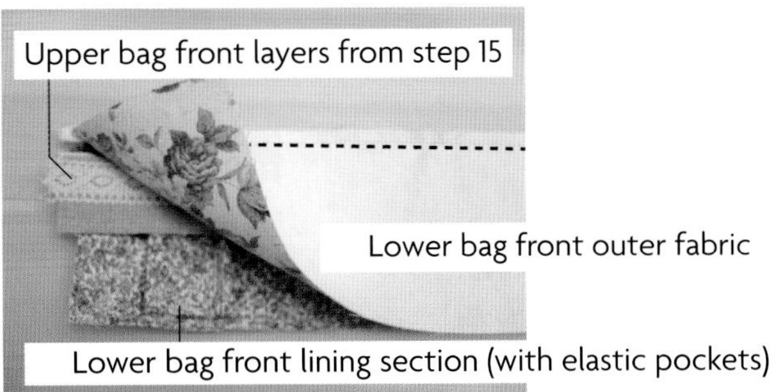

16. Repeat the same procedure for the other side of the zipper tape and the lower bag front pieces.

17. Once the zipper is installed, turn the fabrics right side out and baste the edges together around the perimeter.

18. At this point, the bag is half finished. The upper and lower bag front sections now come together as the bag front, with an outer fabric side and lining fabric side.

19. Take the bag back pieces and trim the interfacing down to 3½" x 5⅛" (9 x 13cm). Iron the interfacing in place, centered in the middle of the fabric.

20. Line up the long edge of the bag back pieces with the bag front layered in between. Lining fabrics should face lining fabric, and outer fabric facing outer fabric.

21. Repeat this same step for the other edge of the bag back and front. You may want to unzip the zipper to make accessing the other bag front edge easier.

22. Turn the fabric right side out, then top stitch the previous seams on the bag back. This completes the outside of the bag, now to be referred to as the bag body.

23. Take the bag bottom outer fabric and align the edges around the bottom edge of the bag body. Sew it in place along a 4¾" (12cm) long section towards the back of the bag body.

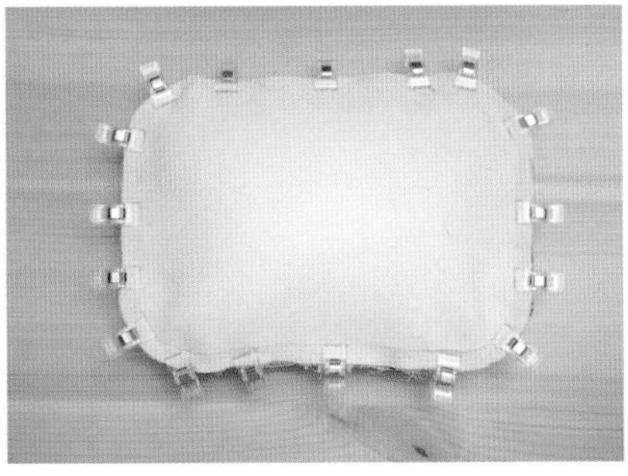

24. Take the bag bottom lining fabric and layer it on the other side of the bag body, lining up the raw edges and facing the right sides together.

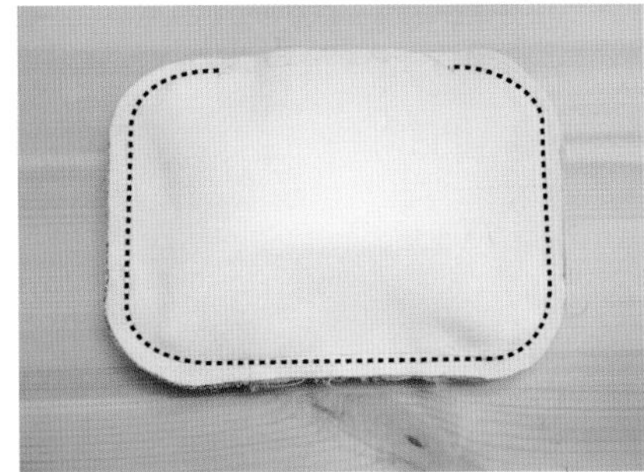

25. Sew the layers together along the edge, skipping over the 4¾" (12cm) section sewn in step 23. This creates the opening for turning the bag right side out.

26. Turn the bag right side out and sew the opening closed.

27. Repeat steps 23–26 with the bag top lining and outer pieces to sew the top of the bag.

28. Attach the leather strap to the top of the bag with rivets.

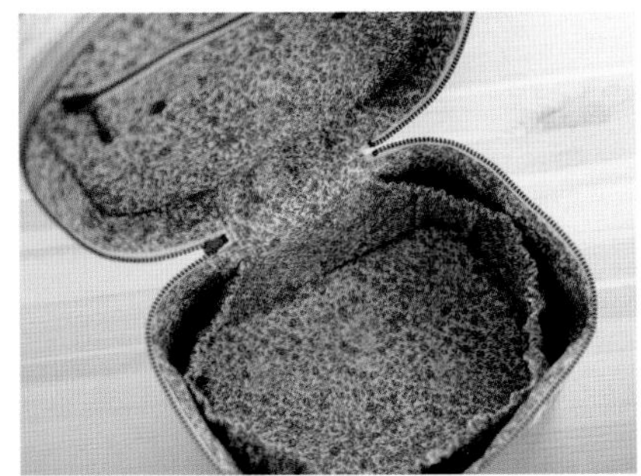

29. Your cute and convenient toiletries bag is now ready to be filled up and taken on the go.

Roomy Tote Bag

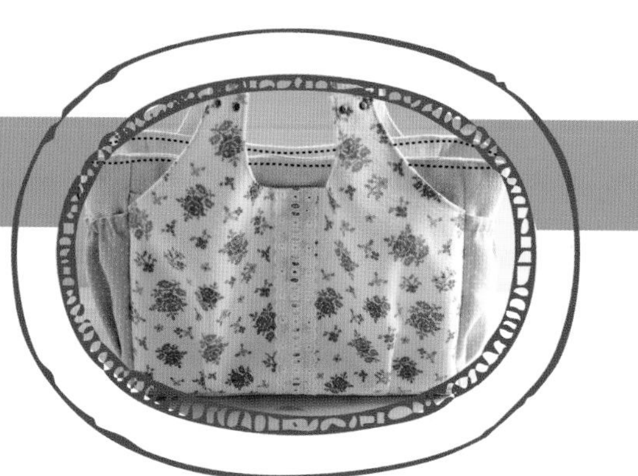

The finished bag measures 14⅛" x 5⅛" x 10⅝" (36 x 13 x 27cm).

Materials:

- ¾ yd. (¾m) of 55" (140cm) wide or 1¼ yd. (1¼m) of 45" (112cm) wide medium-weight fabric for main bag
- ½ yd. (½m) of complementing medium-weight fabric side pockets and shoulder strap
- ½ yd. (½m) of complementing medium-weight fabric for bag cover and handles
- ¾ yd. (¾m) of lightweight fabric for lining
- ¾ yd. (¾m) of complementing lightweight fabric for pockets
- ½ yd. (½m) of 44" (112cm) wide or 1 yd. (1m) of 22" (56cm) wide heavyweight interfacing
- 2¼ yds. (2¼m) of 44" (112cm) wide or 4 yds. (4m) of 22" (56cm) wide lightweight interfacing
- 8" (20cm) zipper
- 16" (40.5cm) zipper
- Magnetic snap
- 2⅓ yds. (2⅓m) of 1⅛" (3cm) wide webbing or similar strap material
- Two 1" (2.5cm) D-rings
- 1" wide strap adjuster
- Two 1" wide lobster clasps

Before you begin:

- Use a ⅜" (1cm) seam allowance unless indicated otherwise.
- Find and trace the 6 pattern pieces from Side A of the pattern paper, remembering to add ⅜" (1cm) seam allowances.
- Note that for the elastic pockets, you may want to bunch up the fabric yourself to get an idea of how much elastic to thread through the pocket. The thickness of your fabric can make a difference.
- Note that the flat pocket in the instructions is made with patchwork of several scraps of fabric. Feel free to mimic the measurements shown in step 12 to achieve the same look.
- Feel free to add extra layers of interfacing to your fabric for more stiffness; just be aware that this will also add to the weight of your bag.
- Note that to get the pattern pieces for the upper bag body and lower bag body for the inner bag, you will need to cut the outer bag body paper pattern along the dotted line indicated in the pattern pack.

Cut the following pieces from your fabric and interfacing:

Note that the interfacing for the bag cover, body, sides, zipper panels, side pockets, and bottom are cut without seam allowances to reduce bulk.

- **Bag Cover** – Outermost layer and handles
    - Bag Cover (A) (from pattern pack): Cover fabric (2), Main fabric (2), Lightweight interfacing (4)
    - Shoulder Strap (B) – cut a 2" x 59" (5 x 150cm) rectangle: Contrast fabric (2)
    - Handles (C) – cut a 3⅜" x 19⅝" (8.5 x 50cm) rectangle: Cover fabric (2)
- **Outer Bag** – Bag sides and layer beneath the bag cover
    - Pocket Strap (D) – cut a 2" x 11⅞" (5 x 30cm) rectangle: Contrast fabric (2)

- Bag Body (E) (from pattern pack): Main fabric (2), Lightweight interfacing (2)
- Outer Side Pockets (F) (from pattern pack): Contrast fabric (2), Lining fabric (2), Lightweight interfacing (2)
- Back Zipper Pocket (G) – cut a 10⅝" x 14⅛" (27 x 36cm) rectangle: Lining fabric (1), Heavyweight interfacing (1)
- Flat Pocket (H) – cut an 11⅞" x 10¼" (30 x 26cm) rectangle: Pocket fabric (1), Heavyweight interfacing (1)
- Three-dimensional Pocket (I) – cut a 17" x 5½" (43 x 14cm) rectangle: Pocket fabric (1), Lining fabric (1), Heavyweight interfacing (1)
- D-Ring Loop (R) – cut a 2⅜" x 2" (6 x 5cm) rectangle: Contrast fabric (1)
- Bag Sides (P) (from pattern pack): Main fabric (2), Heavyweight interfacing (2), Lining fabric (2), Lightweight interfacing (2)
- Bag Bottom (Q) – cut a 15" x 5⅞" (38 x 15cm) rectangle: Main fabric (1), Heavyweight interfacing (2), Lining fabric (1)

- **Inner Bag** – Inner pockets and lining
  - Upper Bag Body (J) (from pattern pack): Main fabric (2), Lightweight interfacing (2)
  - Lower Bag Body (K) (from pattern pack): Lining fabric (2), Lightweight interfacing (2)
  - Top Zipper Panels (L) – cut an 11⅞" x 2⅜" (30 x 6cm) rectangle: Main fabric (2), Lining fabric (2), Lightweight interfacing (2)
  - Zipper Tabs (M) (from pattern pack): Contrast fabric (4)
  - Large Elastic Pockets (N) – cut a 19⅝" x 14⅛" (50 x 36cm) rectangle: Pocket fabric (2), Lightweight interfacing (1)
  - Inner Side Pockets (O) (from pattern pack): Pocket fabric (2), Lining fabric (2), Lightweight interfacing (2)

Instructions

01. For the first inner elastic pocket (N), cut the interfacing to 19⅝" x 6⅝" (50 x 17cm) and refer to Essential Techniques E (pg. 115) for further instructions. Before basting it to the lower bag body (K), make pleats by measuring out left and right from the center vertical line of the pocket. Fold the point at 2⅜" to 1⅛" (6 to 3cm), and then the point from 7" to 8¼" (18 to 21cm). Baste the folds in place.

02. For the second inner elastic pocket (N), repeat the same instructions as for the first pocket, then make the bottom pleats by measuring out from the center vertical line once again. Fold the point at 1½" to 2⅜" (4 to 6cm), the point from 4¾" to 4" (12 to 10cm), and then the point from 7⅞" to 8⅝" (20 to 22cm).

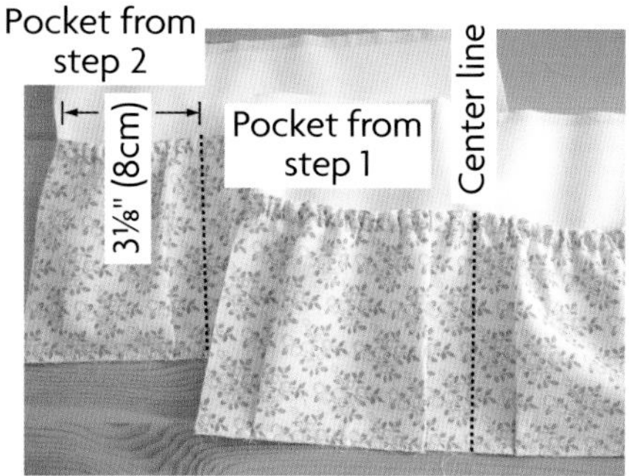

03. Apply the interfacing to the lower bag body pieces (K), then baste the pockets from steps 1 and 2 along the bottom edges. Sew a vertical separation line down the center of the pocket from step 1, while the pocket from step 2 should have two seams 3⅛" (8cm) in from each side edge.

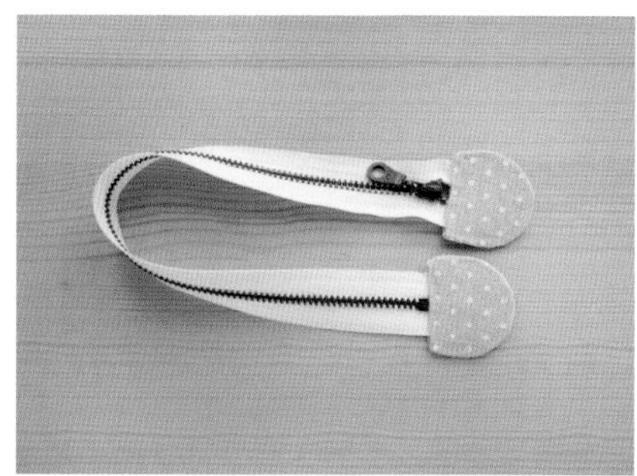

04. To create the zipper tabs, fold under the long edges of the zipper tab pieces by ⅜" (1cm). Layer two of the tab pieces (M) with right sides together, sew the pieces together along the curved edge, trim the seam allowances, and turn the tab right side out. Slip the ends of the zipper into the opening of the tab, then edge stitch around the perimeter of the tab. Repeat this with the last two tab pieces and the other end of the zipper.

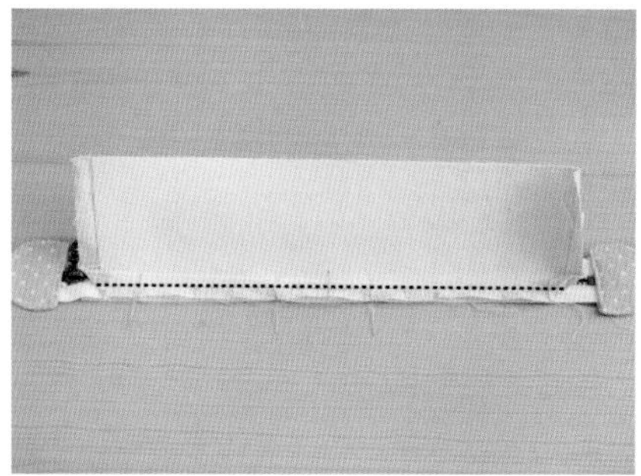

05. Take the top zipper panel pieces (L), trim the interfacing to 11" x 1½" (28 x 4cm), and iron it to the main fabric. Fold under the short edges of the fabrics by ⅜" (1cm), then layer the zipper tape between the long edges of the zipper panel main fabric and lining. Sew all three layers together.

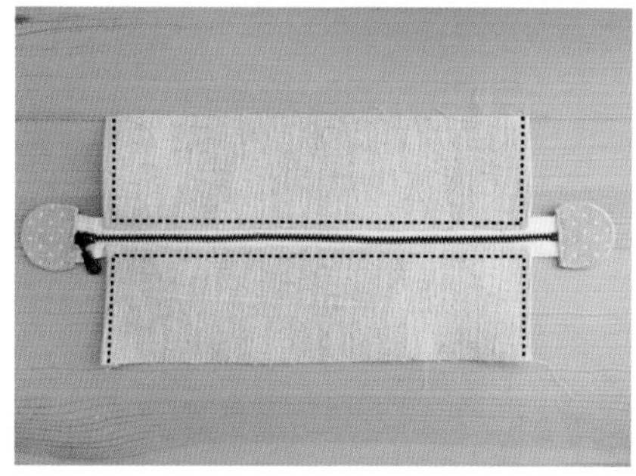

06. Repeat this with the other side of the zipper tape and the remaining top zipper panel pieces. When finished, open out the fabric so the main fabric and zipper is facing upward with the lining beneath it. Edge stitch around the edges of the fabric, over the zipper seams and joining the folded edges along the sides.

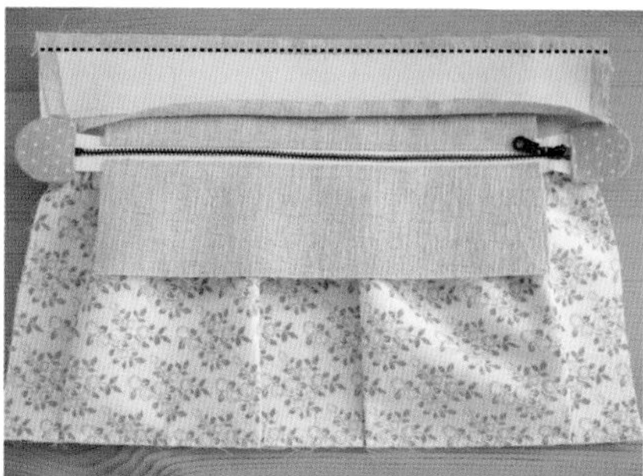

07. Iron the interfacing to the upper bag body (J), then layer the zipper between the bottom edge of the upper bag body and the top edge of the lower bag body (K), centering the zipper between them. Iron the seam allowance towards the upper bag body fabric.

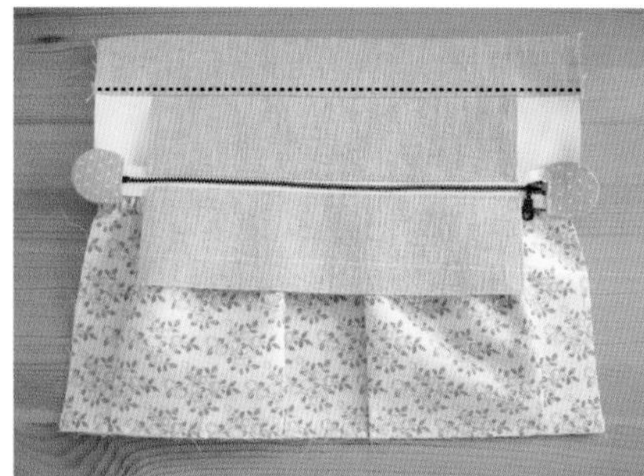

08. Edge stitch the previous seam, then repeat the same instructions for the other side of the zipper panel and the other bag body sections (J and K). This nearly completes the inner bag; this piece will now be referred to as the inner bag body.

09. To create the inner side elastic pockets (O), apply the interfacing, then sew the main fabric to the lining along the upper edge. Refer to Essential Techniques E (pg. 115) to complete the pocket. Create the pleats on the bottom as the pattern guidelines indicate, and baste the edges of the pocket to the bag side lining (P) pieces.

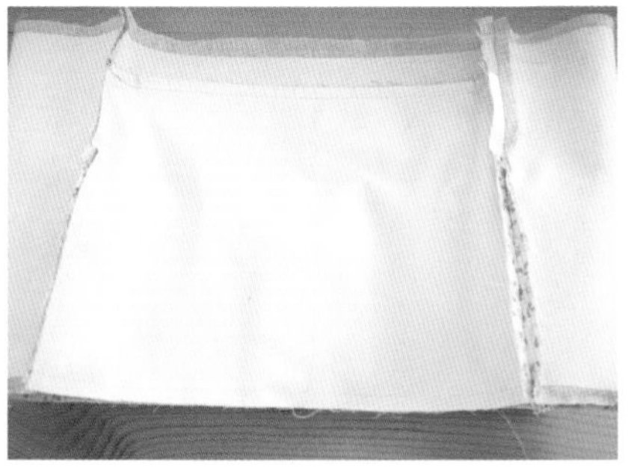

10. Sew the side edges of the bag side lining (P) and inner bag body pieces together, stopping short ⅜" (1cm) before the bottom edge. Continue in this matter attaching the bag sides to the bag body pieces to create a ring.

11. Sew the bottom edge of the inner bag body around the perimeter of the bag bottom lining piece (Q). This finishes the inside of the bag.

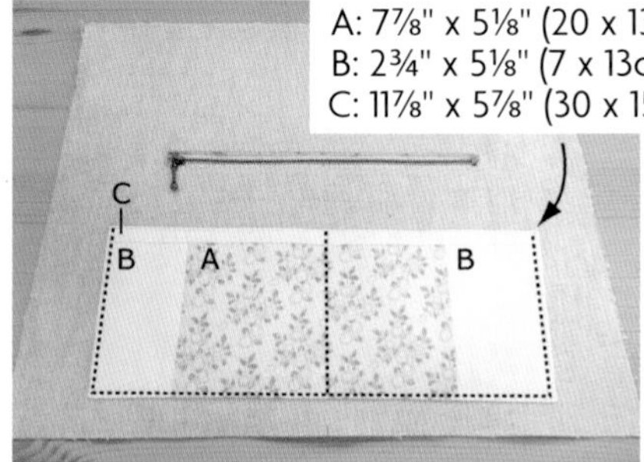

12. To make the flat pocket (H), trim the interfacing to 11" x 4¾" (28 x 12cm) and refer to Essential Techniques C: Version 1 (pg. 110) for instructions. Apply the pocket ¾" (2cm) up from the bottom edge of the outer bag body (E), and edge stitch it in place along the side and bottom edges. Sew a vertical line down the middle to create separate compartments. Then create the zipper pocket following Essential Techniques F (pg. 116).

13. To attach the D-ring, fold under the long edges of the D-ring loop (R) by ⅜" (1cm) and iron the folds in place. Then fold the entire strap in half with wrong sides together, and edge stitch it in place along both sides. Loop the strap around the D-ring, and sew it near the upper left corner of the outer bag body.

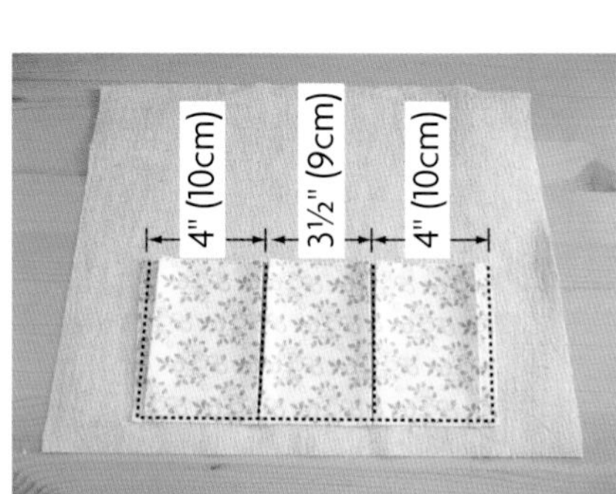

14. To make the three-dimensional pocket (I), trim the interfacing to 16⅛" x 4¾" (41 x 12cm) and refer to Essential Techniques D: Version 1 (pg. 113) for further instructions. Sew pin tucks at 1¾", 3⅜", and 7¼" (4.5, 8.5, and 18.5cm) left and right of the center line. Edge stitch the pocket to the remaining outer bag body (E) ¾" (2cm) up from the bottom edge. Sew it in place along the side and bottom edges of the pocket, as well as vertical separation lines at 1¾" (4.5cm) to the left and right of the center of the pocket.

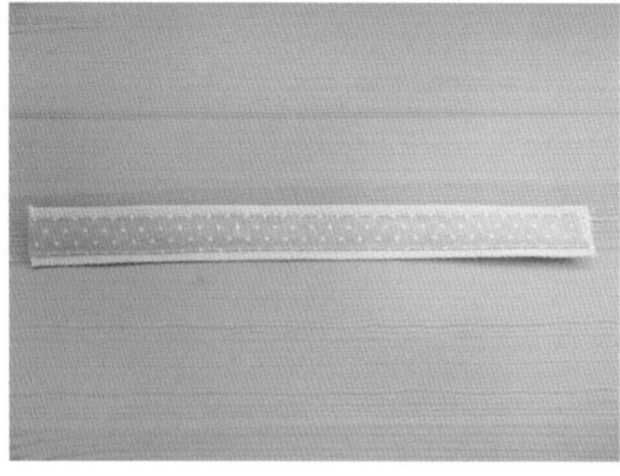

15. Sew the pocket straps (D) together with right sides facing along the long edges. Turn the strap right side out and iron it flat. Cut an 11⅞" (30cm) piece of the webbing material and sew the strap centered on top of the webbing.

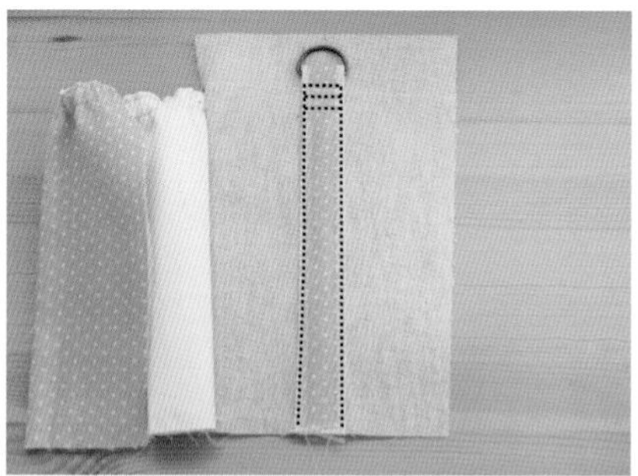

16. Lay the strap centered along the outer bag side (P). Wrap the top edge through a D-ring, then fold under the strap by 1½" (4cm). Edge stitch around the perimeter of the strap, securing it to the bag side and anchoring the D-ring in place with a box stitch.

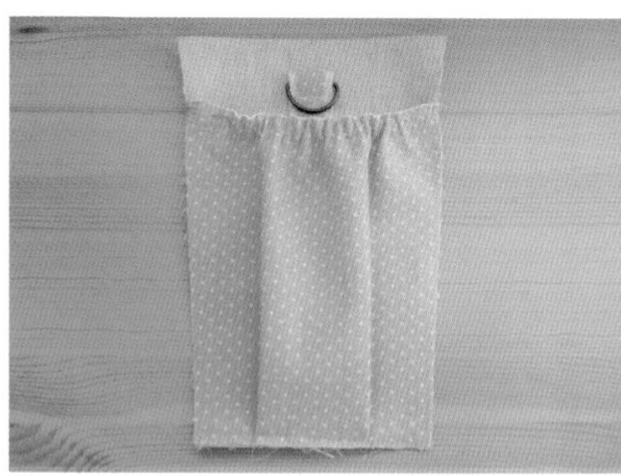

17. Prepare the outer side pockets (F) the same as in step 9, creating the pleats as indicated by the pattern. Then baste the edges to the outer bag sides (P), overlapping the strap from the previous step.

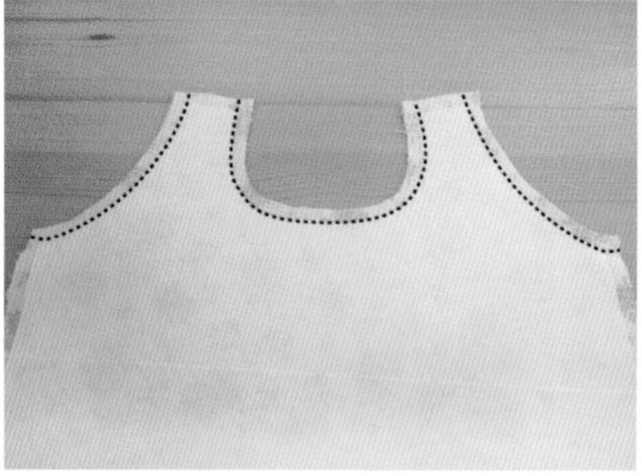

18. Layer the bag cover (A) contrast fabric with its corresponding main fabric piece and sew the top edge together across the rounded edges. Leave the short straight sections free for the handles to come later.

19. Take the handle pieces (C) and fold them in half lengthwise with right sides together. Sew them together along the long edge and turn the handle right side out. Baste the short raw edges together.

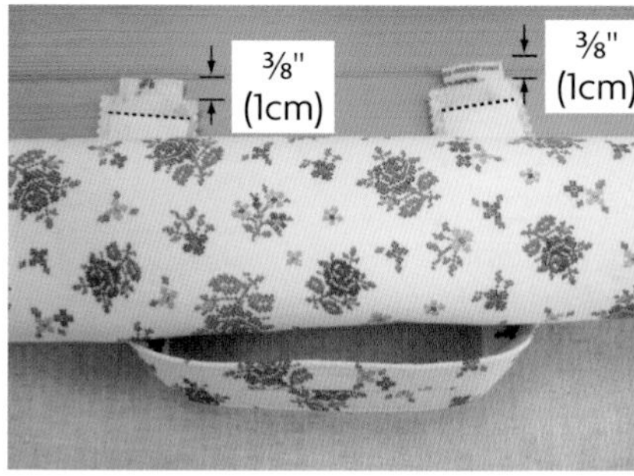

20. Slip the ends of the handle (C) in between the bag cover (A) layers, pushing them through the opening left in step 18. Have the ends of the handle extend by ⅜" (1cm), then sew them in place like a typical seam.

21. Turn the fabric right side out and edge stitch the top edge of the bag cover (A).

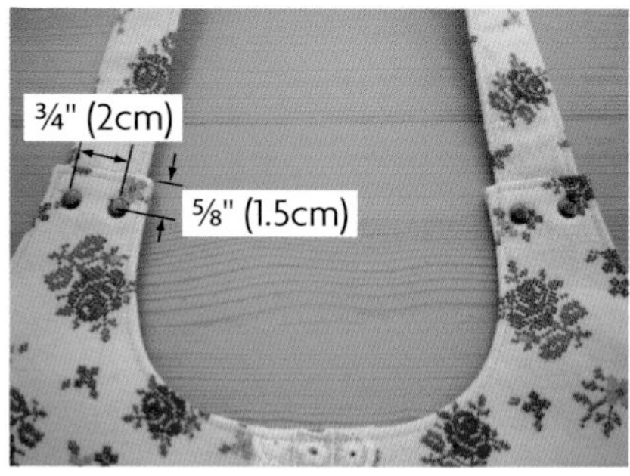

22. To strengthen the handle junction, install two rivets on each side of the handle. Repeat steps 20–22 with the remaining handle piece.

23. Create the pleats at the bottom of the bag cover (A) by folding according to the pattern guidelines. Baste the folds in place.

24. Attach the magnetic snap where the pattern indicates on the outer bag body (E) and the lining of the bag cover (A). See Essential Techniques M (pg. 124) for additional help with this.

25. Line up the sides and bottom edges of the outer bag body (E) and bag cover (A) with both right sides facing up and baste them together.

26. Repeat steps 10 and 11 to attach the outer bag sides (P) and bag bottom (Q) to the bag.

27. Fold under the top edge of the bag lining and outer bag by ⅜" (1cm). Place the bag lining into the outer bag and match up the folded edges, then edge stitch them together. This completes your tote bag.

28. To make the shoulder strap, repeat step 15 with the shoulder strap fabric (B) and remaining section of webbing. Then refer to Essential Techniques I (pg. 120) to complete the adjustable strap with the lobster clasps and strap adjuster.

Book Cover

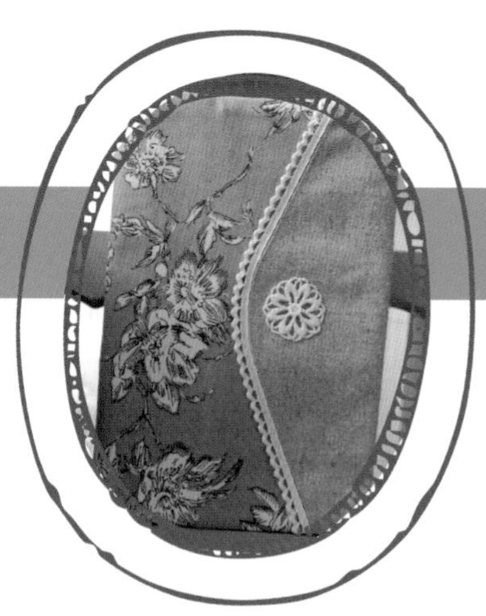

The finished book cover measures 17" x 8⅝" (43 x 22cm).

Materials:

- ⅓ yd. (⅓m) of medium-weight fabric for main cover and bookmark
- ¼ yd. (¼m) of complementing medium-weight fabric for contrast panel
- ⅓ yd. (⅓m) of lightweight fabric for lining
- 6" (18cm) of rickrack
- 10" (25.5cm) of narrow decorative lace
- 10" (25.5cm) of wide decorative lace
- Small decorative lace medallion

Before you begin:

- Use a ⅜" (1cm) seam allowance unless indicated otherwise.
- Find and trace the 3 pattern pieces from Side B of the pattern paper, remembering to add ⅜" (1cm) seam allowances.
- Note that in order to make the cover lining pattern piece, you'll need to overlap the contrast panel and outer cover pattern pieces along the dotted lines.

Cut the following pieces from your fabric:

- **Contrast Panel** (from pattern pack): Contrast fabric (1)
- **Outer Cover** (from pattern pack): Main outer fabric (1)
- **Cover Lining** (from pattern pack): Lining fabric (1)
- **Bookmark** (from pattern pack): Main outer fabric (2)

01. Gather your two bookmark pieces and the 7" (18cm) length of rickrack.

02. Layer the bookmark pieces right sides together with the rickrack sandwiched in between them along the point. Sew around the perimeter of the bookmark, leaving a 1⅛" (3cm) space along the bottom edge.

03. Turn the bookmark right side out and iron it flat, then edge stitch around the entire perimeter of the bookmark.

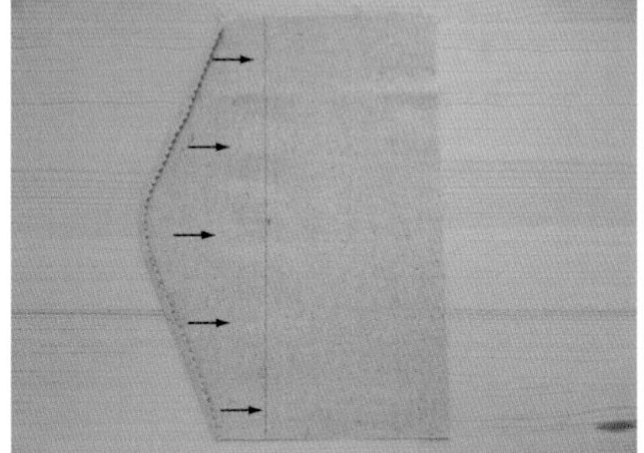

04. Take the contrast panel and sew a zigzag stitch along the curved edge at the side. Line up the paper pattern (without seam allowances) over the fabric and use it to iron the zigzagged edge against the paper to fold it over cleanly.

05. Layer the contrast panel over the outer cover (with both right sides facing up) according to the pattern guidelines. Edge stitch the panel in place, then cover the seam with the decorative lace. Also sew on the lace medallion.

06. Following the pattern guidelines, baste the lace and bookmark rickrack onto the outer cover along the outer edges. This finishes the outer book cover.

07. Layer the lining over the outer cover with right sides facing. Match up the short straight edges and sew them together along this edge.

08. Turn the fabric right side out and edge stitch the previous seam $\frac{1}{16}$" (0.2cm) from the edge. Fold the two fabrics along the line indicated by the pattern and iron the fold in place.

09. Fold the fabric back with right sides together, then tuck the edge stitched side inward to go along with the folds from the previous step. The result should resemble a $\sum$ shape.

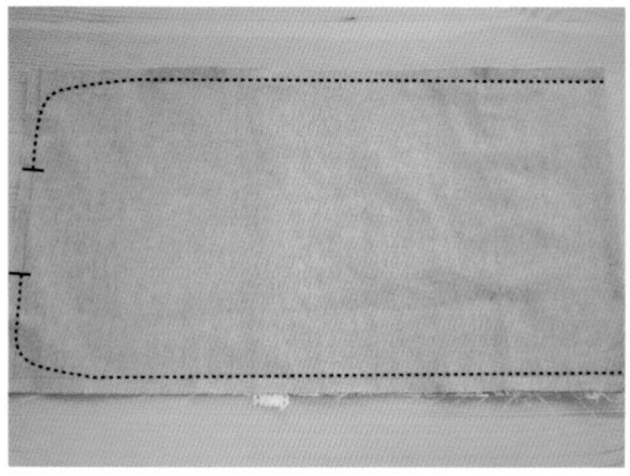

10. Sew around the perimeter of the cover, leaving an opening on the left side for turning the cover right side out.

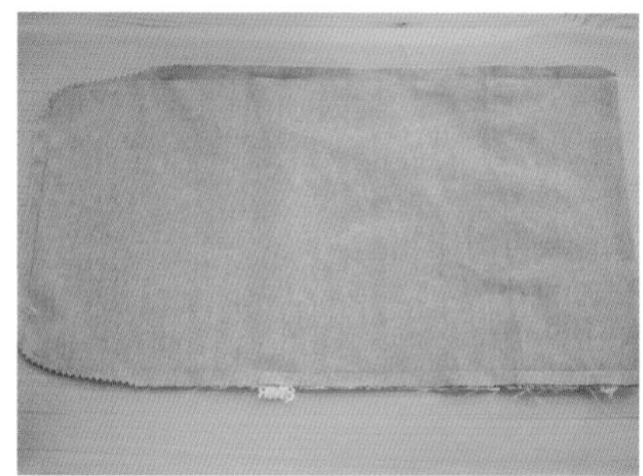

11. Trim the corners and seam allowances with pinking shears.

12. Turn the cover right side out and iron it flat. Sew the opening closed.

13. This completes your book cover.

Cell Phone Sleeve

The finished cell phone sleeve measures 5⅜" x 3⅛" (13.5 x 8cm).

Materials:

- ¼ yd. (¼m) of medium to heavyweight fabric for main case – Fabric A
- ⅛ yd. (⅛m) of complementing medium to heavyweight fabric for contrast panel – Fabric B
- ¼ yd. (¼m) of lightweight fabric for lining
- ¼ yd. (¼m) of fusible fleece interfacing
- Two metal sew-in snaps
- Small decorative cloth patch

Before you begin:

- Use a ⅜" (1cm) seam allowance unless indicated otherwise.
- Find and trace the 1 pattern piece from Side B of the pattern paper, remembering to add ⅜" (1cm) seam allowances.

Cut the following pieces from your fabric:

Note that the interfacing is cut without seam allowances to reduce bulk.

- **Side Panels** – cut a 2¾" x 9½" (7 x 24cm) rectangle: Main outer fabric – A (2)
- **Center Panel** – cut a 2⅜" x 9½" (6 x 24cm) rectangle: Contrast fabric – B (1)
- **Case Lining** (from pattern pack): Lining fabric (1), Fusible fleece interfacing (1)

Instructions

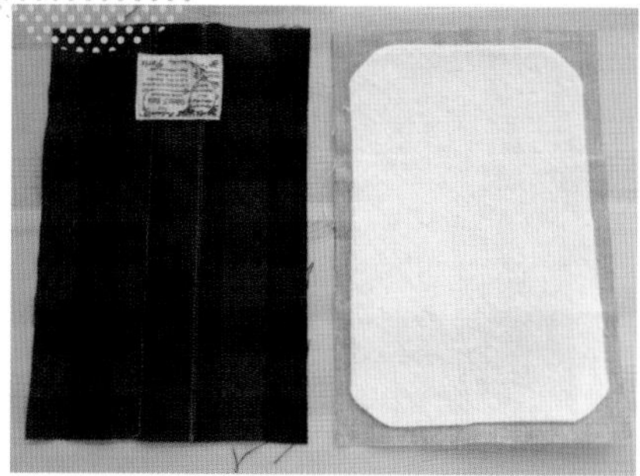

01. Sew the strips of the outer fabrics A and B along their long edges to create a row with fabric A on the outside panels and fabric B in the middle. Apply the decorative patch. Iron the fusible fleece interfacing to the wrong side of the lining fabric – note that the seam allowances are cut off.

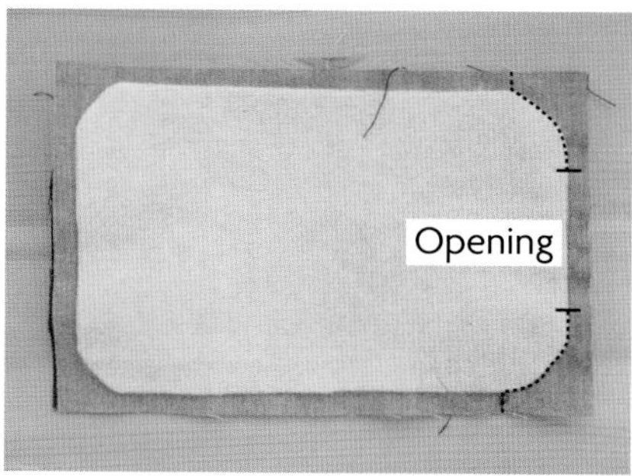

02. Layer the outer fabric and lining together with right sides facing. Sew a seam along the short side of the case opposite to the edge where the patch is located, but leave an opening according to the pattern guidelines.

03. Turn the fabric right side out and iron the seam. Then tuck the fabric inward to create folds along the dotted lines indicated by the pattern. The resulting shape should resemble a $\sum$ symbol.

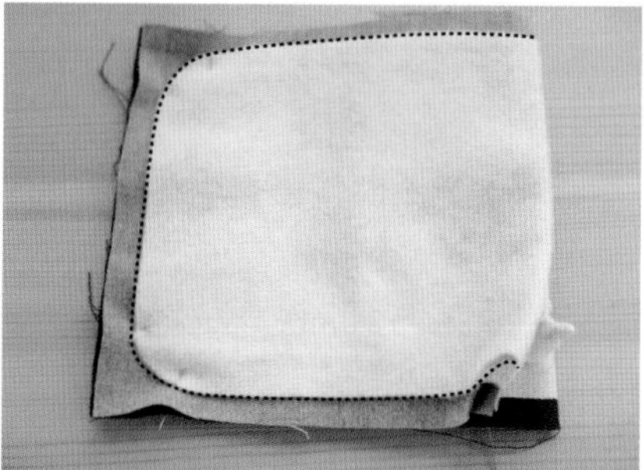

04. While the fabric is folded, sew along the top, bottom, and one side edge.

05. Trim the seam allowances and turn the case right side out. Sew the opening closed and attach the metal snap prongs along the upper corners of the lining. Fold the case around your phone and attach the metal snap sockets where the prongs line up onto the outer fabric.

06. You have now finished your cell phone sleeve.

Mini Binder

The finished large binder measures 5½" x 7½" (14 x 19cm), and the small binder measures 4⅛" x 6¼" (10.5 x 16cm).

Materials:

- ¼ yd. (¼m) of medium-weight fabric for binder and flap
- ¼ yd. (¼m) of complementing light to medium-weight fabric for flap
- ¼ yd. (¼m) of lightweight fabric for lining
- ¼ yd. (¼m) of 44" (112cm) wide or ⅓ yd. (⅓m) of 22" (56cm) wide heavyweight interfacing
- ¼ yd. (¼m) of ultra-firm fusible interfacing
- 11" x 7½" (28 x 19cm) (large) or 8¼" x 6⅜" (21 x 16cm) (small) piece of chipboard or plastic sheet
- Magnetic button
- Two metal rivets
- Six-ring loose-leaf binder spine (small, for 3" x 5" [7.5 x 12.5cm] sheets; or large, for 3¾" x 6¾" [9.5 x 17cm] sheets)
- 13¾" (35cm) of wide decorative lace
- 4¾" (12cm) of narrow decorative lace
- Small decorative lace medallion

Before you begin:

- Use a ⅜" (1cm) seam allowance unless indicated otherwise.
- Before cutting and making the front flap, please read Essential Techniques B: Version 2 (pg. 109).
- You can buy a six-ring loose-leaf binder spine at many stationery or leather supply stores. Make sure that the thickness and length of the binder spine you choose matches up with the measurements of your notebook.
- Chipboard is a hard paper backing that will help to make your binder sturdier. You can also substitute a plastic sheet; just be sure to cut the plastic ¼" (0.5cm) smaller than the measurements for the chipboard.
- Find and trace the 3 pattern pieces from Side A of the pattern paper, remembering to add ⅜" (1cm) seam allowances. Note that the chipboard pieces follow the pattern shape but do not need a seam allowance.

Cut the following pieces from your fabric and interfacing:

Note that for the binder and flap the interfacing is cut without seam allowances to reduce bulk.

- **Binder Flap:**
  - Top Layer (from pattern pack): Main outer fabric (1), Lining fabric (1), Heavyweight interfacing (1)
  - Bottom Layer (from pattern pack): Contrast fabric (2), Heavyweight interfacing (1)
- **Binder Cover** (from pattern pack: choose either small or large): Main outer fabric (1), Lining fabric (1), Ultra-firm interfacing (1), Heavyweight interfacing (1)
- **Binder Backing** (from pattern pack: choose either small or large): Chipboard (1) OR Plastic sheet (1) with ¼" (0.5cm) trimmed off each edge
- **Pocket** – cut a 4¾" x 4¾" (12 x 12cm) square: Lining fabric (1), Heavyweight interfacing (1)

Instructions

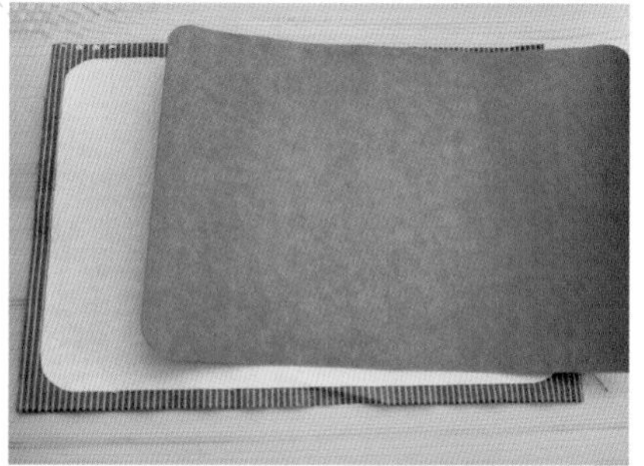

01. Iron the ultra-firm interfacing onto the outer binder fabric and cut the chipboard to fit over it.

02. Using a hot glue gun, attach the chipboard to the outer fabric. Iron it to get any bumps out. If you use a plastic sheet instead of chipboard, adhere it to the outer fabric with double-sided adhesive tape.

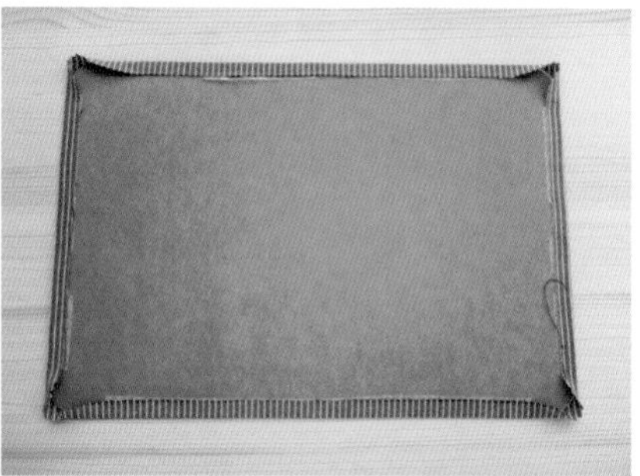

03. Fold down the outer fabric sides and glue them to the chipboard, leaving the corners for the next step. Iron down the sides to secure them in place.

04. To round the corners, run a short gathering stitch across the corner fabric to bunch it up. Then glue the fabric with a hot glue gun. Iron it flat to secure the fabric.

05. Repeat this with all four corners.

06. Sew the wide decorative lace along the bottom edge of the binder, folding the excess towards the inside.

07. Repeat steps 4–5 for the binder lining after applying the interfacing.

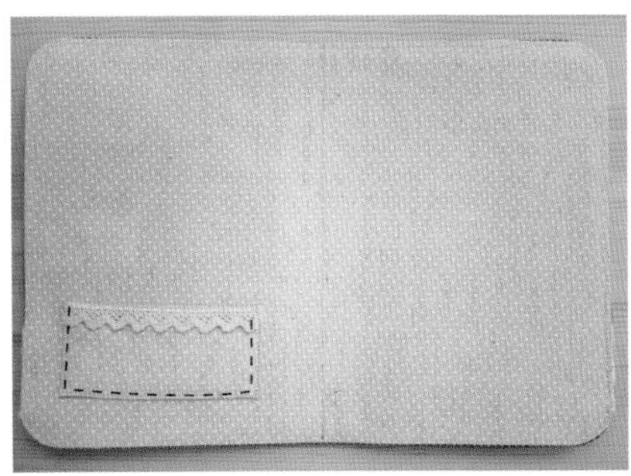

08. Trim the pocket interfacing to 4" x 2" (10 x 5cm) and apply it to the pocket fabric. See Essential Techniques C: Version 1 (pg. 110) to complete the pocket. Sew the narrow decorative lace to the top edge, then edge stitch the pocket along the sides and bottom to the binder lining.

09. Refer to Essential Techniques B: Version 2 (pg. 109) to create the binder flap. Attach the magnetic button.

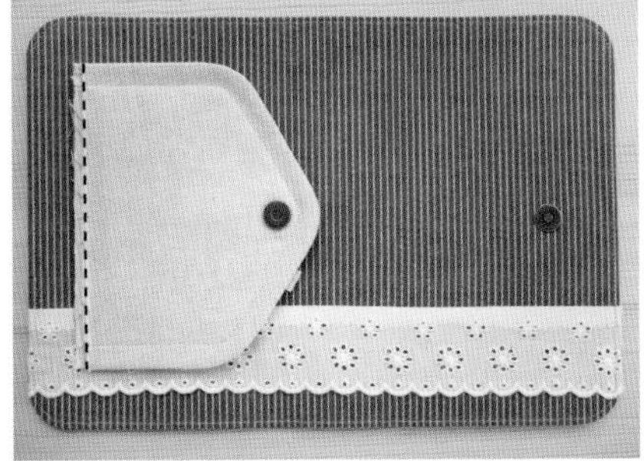

10. Align the flap over the outer binder 1⅛" (3cm) in from the left edge. Sew the flap in place ¼" (0.5cm) in from the raw edge.

11. Align the inner and outer binder sections together with wrong sides facing. Edge stitch completely around the perimeter to secure the two pieces in together.

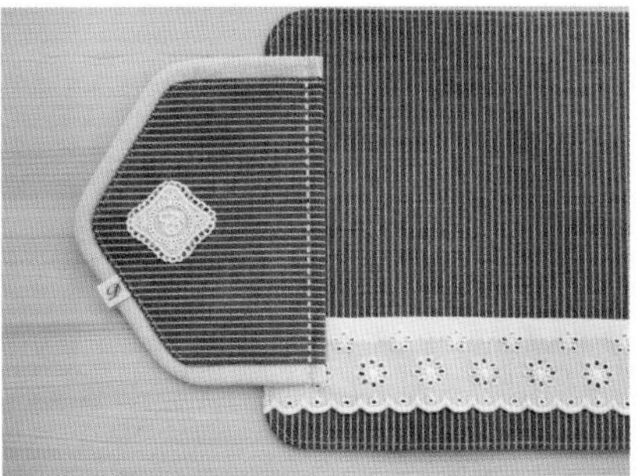

12. Fold the flap downward and sew it in place 5⁄16" (0.7cm) away from the fold. This completes the binder flap.

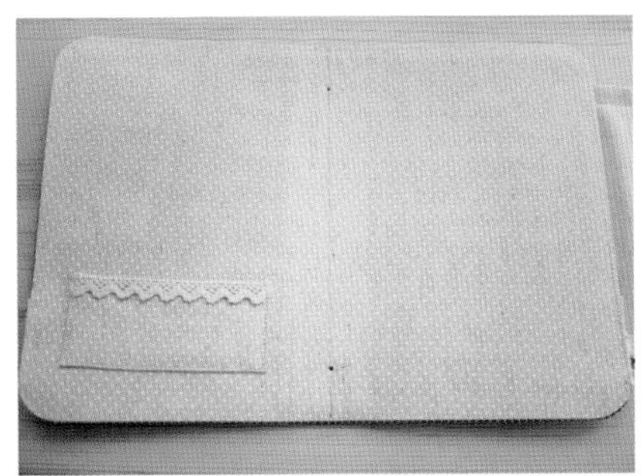

13. Find the center vertical line of the binder inside the lining. Position the six-ring loose-leaf binder spine over this line to find the proper placement. Mark the placement with a hole punch.

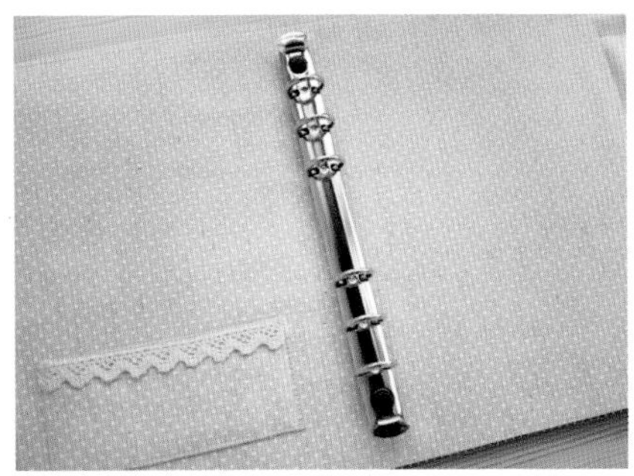

14. Attach the six-ring loose-leaf binder spine with metal rivets where the marks were made in the previous step.

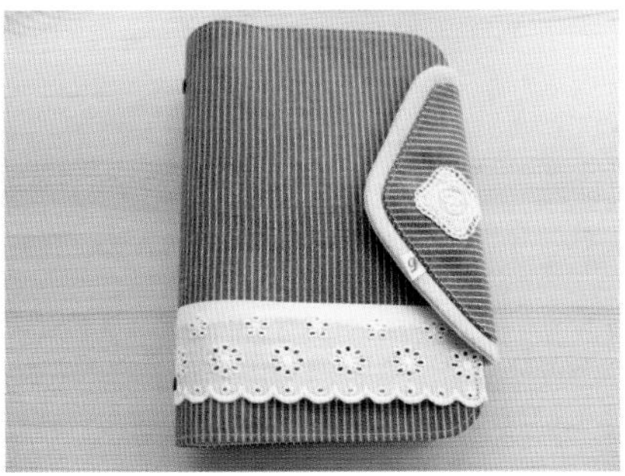

15. You have finished your mini binder.

Passport Case

The finished passport case measures 4¾" x 5⅞" (12 x 15cm).

Materials:

- ¼ yd. (¼m) of medium-weight fabric for outer cover center panel
- ¼ yd. (¼m) of complementing medium-weight fabric for outer cover side panels
- ¼ yd. (¼m) of lightweight fabric for lining
- ¼ yd. (¼m) of 44" (112cm) wide or ⅓ yd. (⅓m) of 22" (56cm) wide heavyweight interfacing
- 14" (35.5cm) of wide decorative lace
- 16" (40.5cm) zipper
- Decorative metal medallion

Before you begin:

- Use a 5⁄16" (0.7cm) seam allowance unless indicated otherwise.
- Find and trace the 1 pattern piece from Side A of the pattern paper, remembering to add 5⁄16" (0.7cm) seam allowances.

Cut the following pieces from your fabric and interfacing:

Note that the interfacing is cut without seam allowances to reduce bulk.

- **Outer Cover:**
  - Center Panel – cut an 8" x 6¾" (20.5 x 17cm) rectangle: Main outer fabric (1)
  - Side Panels – cut a 1¾" x 6¾" (4.5 x 17cm) rectangle: Contrast fabric (2)
- **Case Lining** (from pattern pack): Lining fabric (1), Heavyweight interfacing (1)
- **Pockets Side A** – cut a 10⅝" x 6⅝" (27 x 17cm) rectangle: Lining fabric (1)
- **Side A Interfacing** – cut a 7⅛" x 6⅛" (18 x 15.5cm) rectangle: Heavyweight interfacing (1)
- **Pockets Side B** – cut an 11" x 6⅝" (28 x 17cm) rectangle: Lining fabric (1)
- **Side B Interfacing** – cut a 3⅜" x 6⅛" (8.5 x 15.5cm) rectangle: Heavyweight interfacing (1)

01. Join the center panel to the two side panels along the 6¾" (17cm) edges. The finished fabric should have the center panel between the two side panels in one large rectangle. Apply the wide decorative lace along the finished seams. Iron the cover lining interfacing pieces and the cover lining piece to the back of this fabric.

02. Trim around the edges of the cover front interfacing, adding a 5⁄16" (0.7cm) seam allowance.

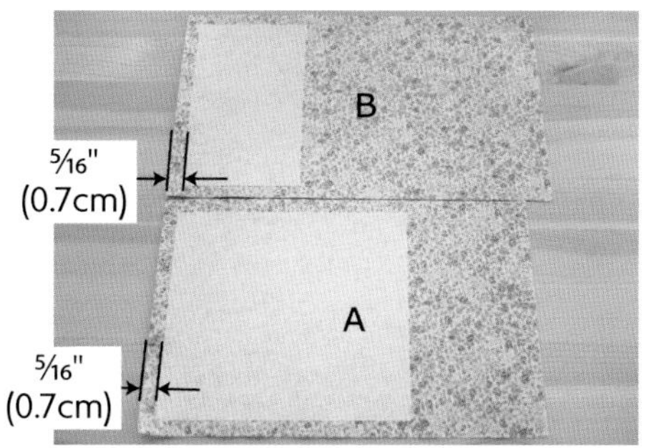

03. Iron the pocket interfacing to the corresponding fabric pieces. Align them towards one side of the fabric, 5⁄16" (0.7cm) in from the edge.

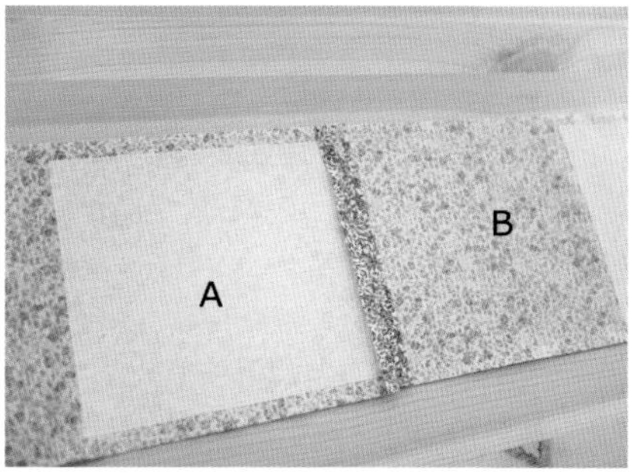

04. Line up the pocket pieces together along the 6¾" (17cm) edges. After making sure that the interfaced end of piece A is lined up with the non-interfaced end of piece B, sew the edges together.

05. Lay the A and B fabrics so the right sides are facing and sew the remaining side seam.

06. Turn the fabrics right side out and iron them. With side A facing up, tuck under the fabric on the side without interfacing. Make a fold against the edge of the interfacing from sides A and B. The fabric should naturally want to fold along this edge due to the resistance from the interfacing; iron the fold in place.

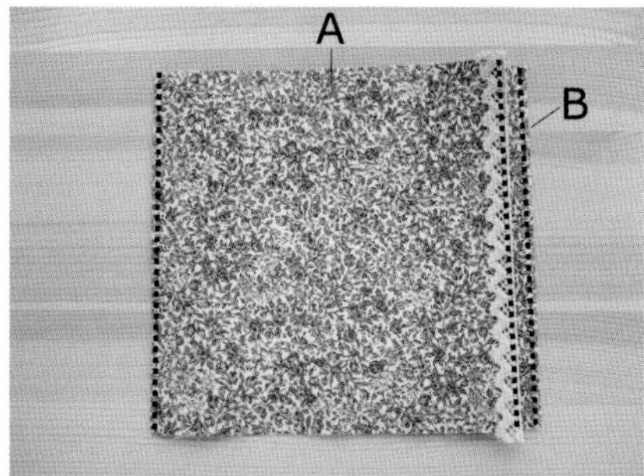

07. Sew the decorative lace along the right (folded) edge of the A fabric. Edge stitch the fold on the left side of the fabric as well as the fold on the right side (from the B fabric) as indicated in the picture.

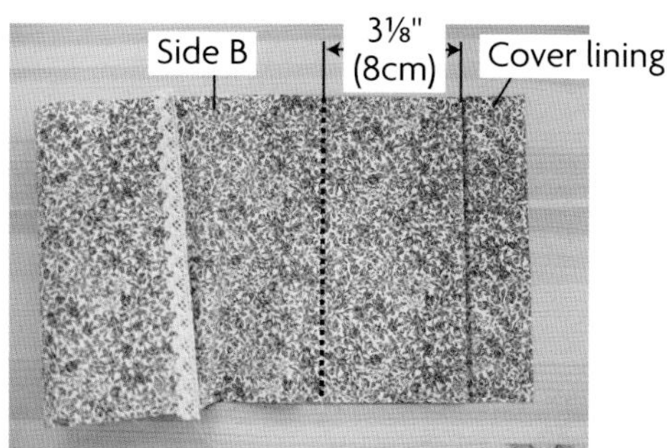

08. Lay the pockets centered over the cover lining with both right sides facing up. Lift up side A of the pocket fabric and sew a vertical seam 3⅛" (8cm) in from the folded edge of side B.

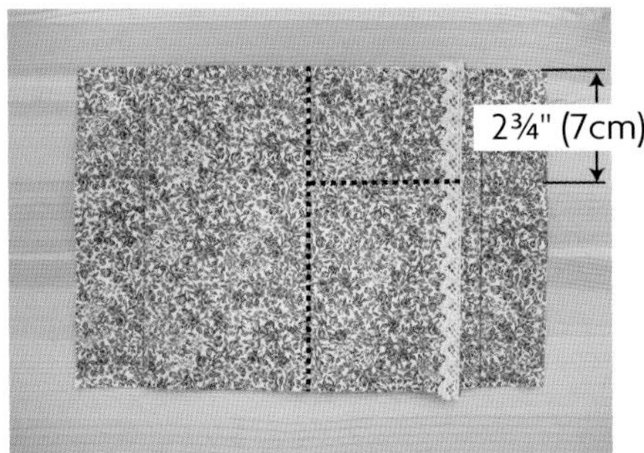

09. Fold side A back to where it was before (overlapping side B) and sew a vertical seam along the center line. Then, on the right side, sew a horizontal seam 2¾" (7cm) down from the top edge, going through the two pocket layers to create the card pocket. This completes the pocket section of the cover.

10. Take the outer cover from step 1 and apply fusible web tape or fabric glue along the seam allowances of the cover on the right side.

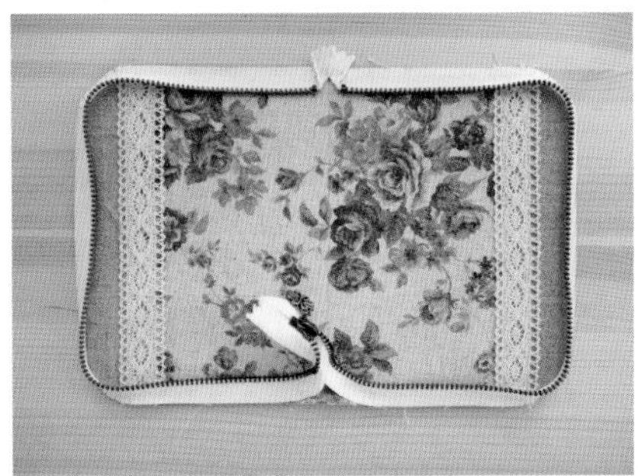

11. Lay the zipper around the perimeter of the outer cover, making sure that the end of the zipper extends into the middle of the cover and the head of the zipper extends out by ⅝" (1.5cm). Fuse the zipper tape in place, then baste it along the outer edges.

12. Clip the zipper tape around the corners so it curves more smoothly, but be sure not to clip more than the 5⁄16" (0.7cm) seam allowance.

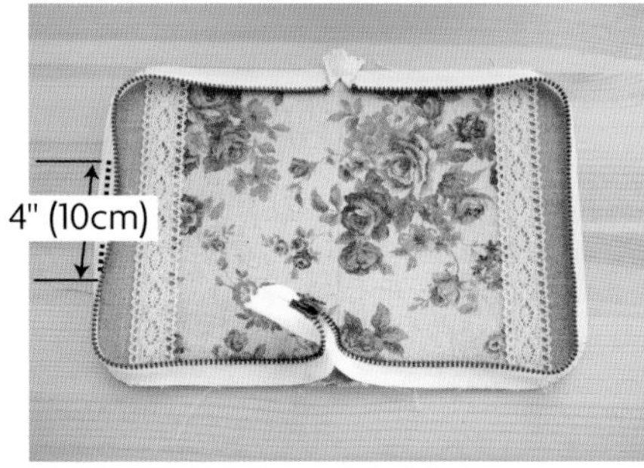

13. On the left side, sew a 4" (10cm) seam along the zipper tape.

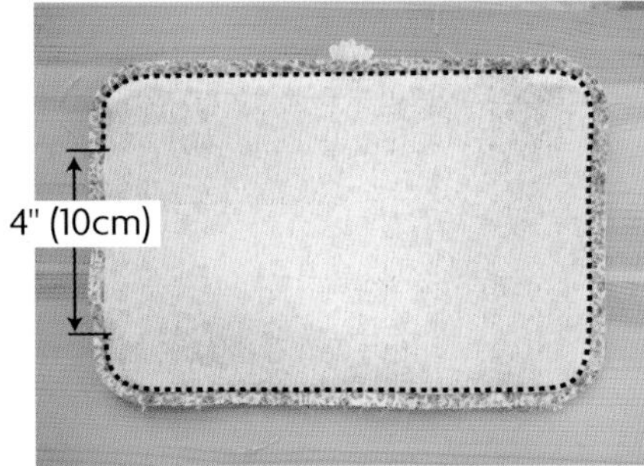

14. Line up the lining fabric over the outer cover fabric and sew them together around the perimeter, skipping over the 4" (10cm) section that was sewn previously, which will be the opening for turning the cover right side out.

15. Trim the seam allowances and turn the cover right side out. Sew the opening closed. You may want to flip the end of the zipper to the inside of the cover and hand sew it in place to the lining.

16. Sew on the decorative metal medallion, and you have completed your passport case.

Notebook Cover

The finished notebook cover measures 7" x 8⅝" (18 x 22cm) and fits an A5-sized notebook or binder.

Materials:

- ⅓ yd. (⅓m) of medium to heavyweight fabric for main cover – Fabric A
- ⅛ yd. (⅛m) of complementing medium to heavyweight fabric for contrast panel – Fabric B
- ⅓ yd. (⅓m) of lightweight fabric for lining
- Leather bound metal snap
- Small decorative cloth patch

Before you begin:

- Use a ⅜" (1cm) seam allowance unless indicated otherwise.
- Note that the placement of the pencil pocket, flap, and separation lines in step 5 can be changed according to your needs, as long as they are still within the fold line.

Cut the following pieces from your fabric:

- **Outer Cover:**
  - Side Panels – cut a 2¾" x 9½" (31 x 25cm) rectangle: Main outer fabric – A (2)
  - Center Panel – cut a 2⅜" x 9½" (11 x 25cm) rectangle: Contrast fabric – B (1)
- **Cover Lining** – cut a 27⅛" x 9⅞"(69 x 25cm) rectangle: Lining fabric (1)
- **Pencil Pocket and Flap** – cut a 7⅞" x 5½" (20 x 14cm) rectangle: Main outer fabric (1), Lining fabric (1)

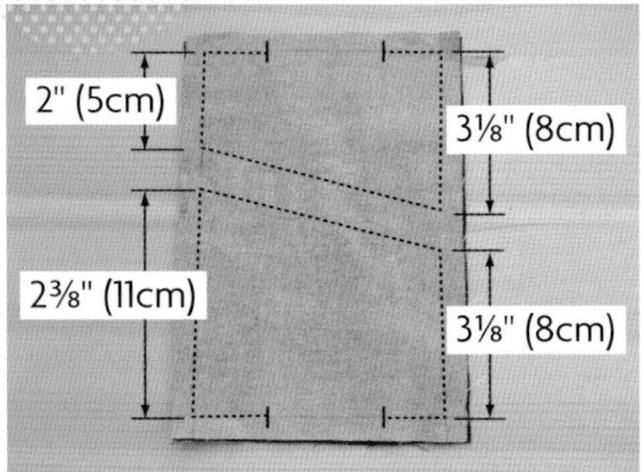

01. Layer the pencil pocket outer fabric and lining together with right sides facing. Following the measurements in the photograph, sew along the edges of the pocket, leaving an opening at the top and bottom. Sew slanted lines to separate the pocket halves.

02. Cut the pocket in half between the slanted seams, then iron the seams flat.

03. Turn the pockets right side out and iron them flat. Edge stitch along the sides and slanted edges of the smaller pocket half (pocket flap). Edge stitch only along the slanted edge of the larger pocket half (pencil pocket).

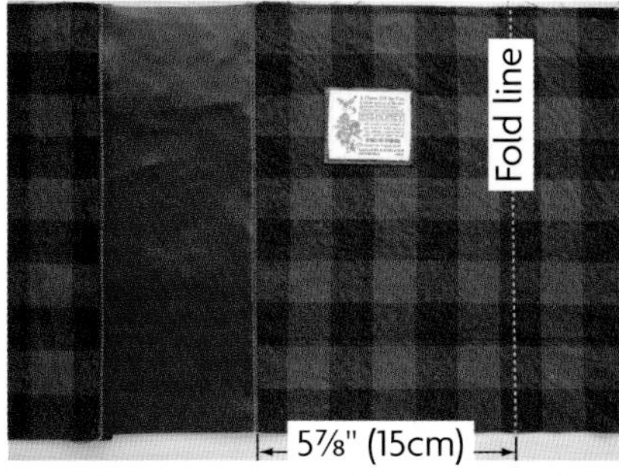

04. Sew the outer fabrics A and B together along the 9⅞" (25cm) edges, creating a row with the fabric A pieces as the side panels and the fabric B piece as the center panel in between. Sew on the decorative patch, then mark the fold lines of the cover, 5⅞" (15cm) out to the left and right from the center panel of fabric B.

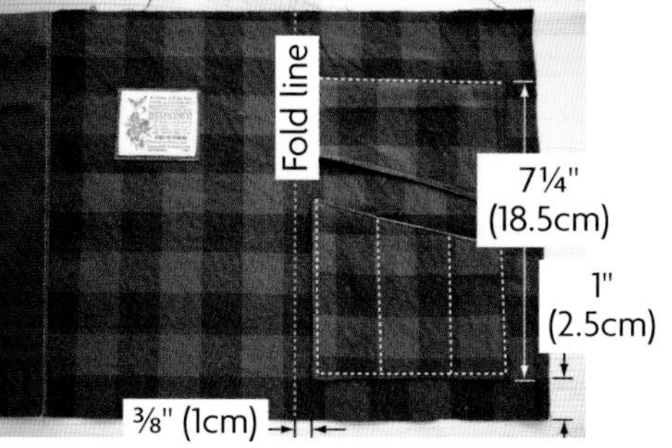

05. Line up the pencil pocket 1" (2.5cm) above and ⅜" (1cm) to the right of the fold line from the previous step. Line up the flap 1" (2.5cm) above the pocket, so the entire section is about 7¼"(18.5cm). Edge stitch the pocket in place along the sides and bottom, and edge stitch the flap in place along the top. Sew separating lines about 1¼" (3.3cm) along the width of the pocket.

06. Attach the leather snap centered just inside the fold lines. This finishes the outside of the notebook cover.

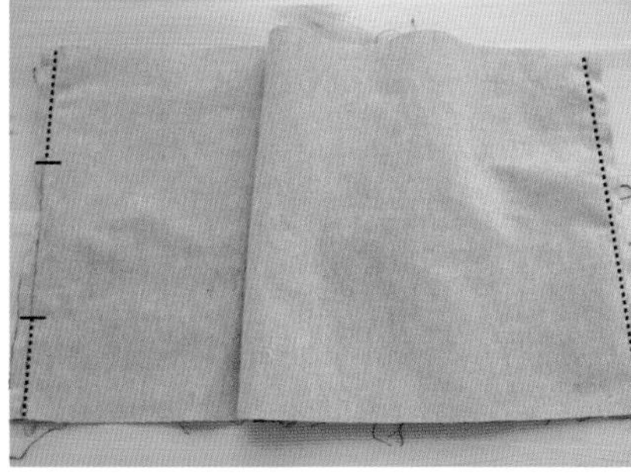

07. Layer the outer cover over the lining, matching up the raw edges. Sew them together along the side edges, leaving a 4" (10cm) opening centered along one side. Iron the seams.

08. Turn the cover right side out and edge stitch the seam without the opening.

09. Fold the side seams of the cover inward along the fold lines established previously, to resemble a ∑ shape. Flatten the fabric out while it's folded as such, then sew the upper and lower raw edges.

10. Turn the fabric right side out through the opening in the side. Edge stitch the remaining side edge to close up the opening.

11. Insert a notebook or a small binder in the center of the notebook cover.

12. You have finished your notebook cover.

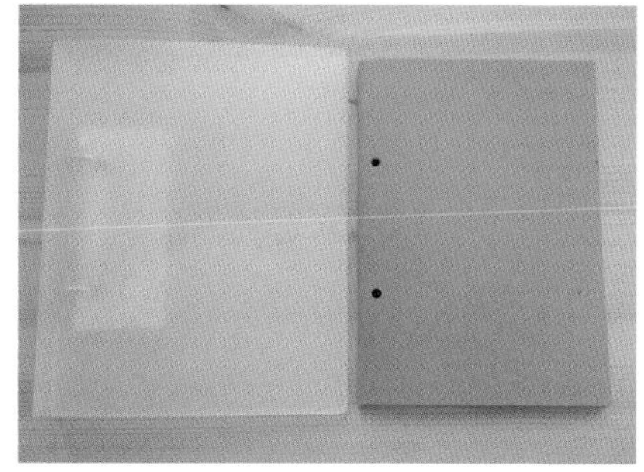

13. The notebook used here was a two-hole A5 binder for holding A5-sized notebooks.

Card Case

The finished card case measures 3½" x 3⅛" (9 x 8cm).

Materials:

- ⅛ yd. (⅛m) of medium-weight fabric for case top panel
- ⅛ yd. (⅛m) of complementing medium-weight fabric for case bottom panel
- ¼ yd. (¼m) of lightweight fabric for lining
- ¼ yd. (¼m) of heavyweight interfacing
- Monogrammed ribbon
- 7½" (19cm) of wide decorative lace
- Plastic credit card wallet insert
- Leather strap with attached snap

Before you begin:

- Use a ⅜" (1cm) seam allowance unless indicated otherwise.
- Find and trace the 2 pattern pieces from Side A of the pattern paper, remembering to add ⅜" (1cm) seam allowances.

Cut the following pieces from your fabric and interfacing:

Note that the interfacing is cut without seam allowances to reduce bulk.

- **Outer Case:**
  - Top Panel – cut a 7" x 4" (18 x 10cm) rectangle: Main outer fabric (1)
  - Bottom Panel – cut a 7" x 2" (18 x 5cm) rectangle: Contrast fabric (1)
- **Case Lining** (from pattern pack): Lining fabric (1), Heavyweight interfacing (1)
- **Pockets** (from pattern pack): Lining fabric (4), Heavyweight interfacing (4)

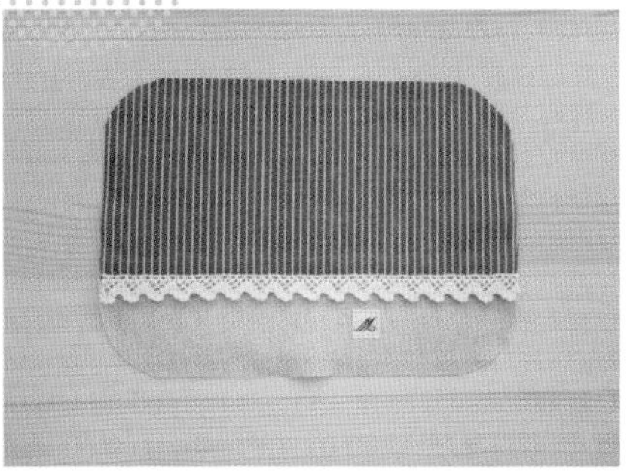

01. For the outer case, sew the upper panel to the lower panel, matching up the long edges. When finished, sew the decorative lace along the seam and attach the monogrammed ribbon. Iron the case lining interfacing to the outer case fabric, then trim the fabric around the interfacing, adding the usual ⅜" (1cm) seam allowance.

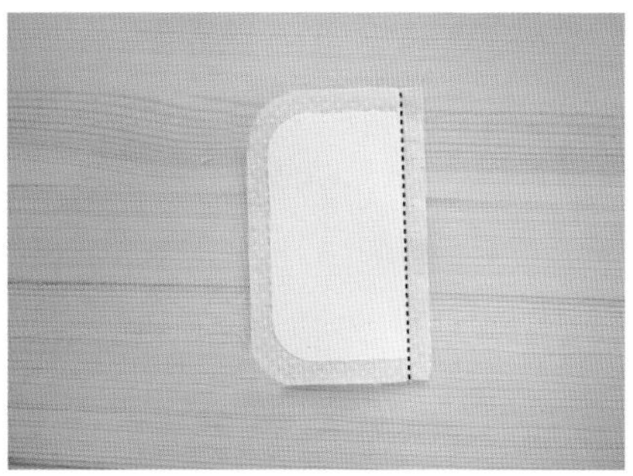

02. Iron the interfacing to the pocket pieces and sew two of them together along the long straight edge with right sides facing. Fold the fabric back right side out and baste the raw edges together. Repeat this with the remaining two pocket pieces.

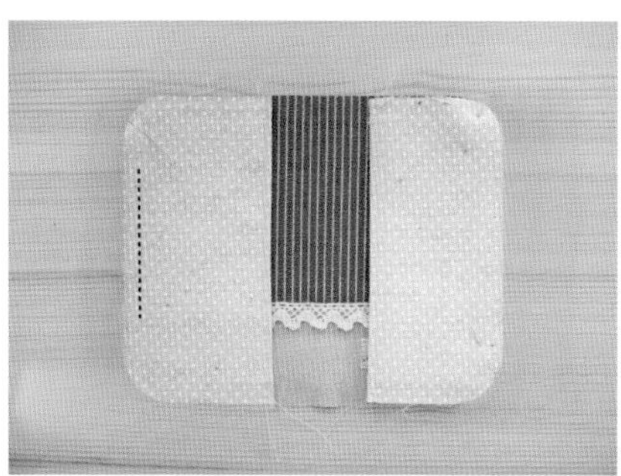

03. Align the raw edges of the pockets along the sides of the outer case with right sides together. Sew a 2" (5cm) seam along one side edge.

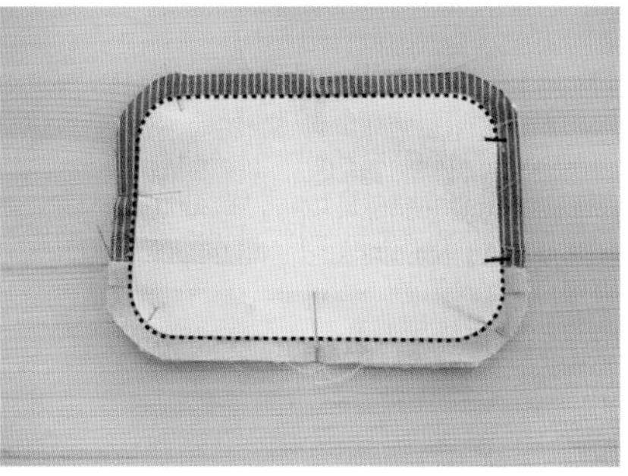

04. Layer the outer case fabric over the lining with right sides together. Sew them together around the perimeter of the fabric, skipping over the 2" (5cm) section sewn previously. This is to leave an opening to turn the case right side out.

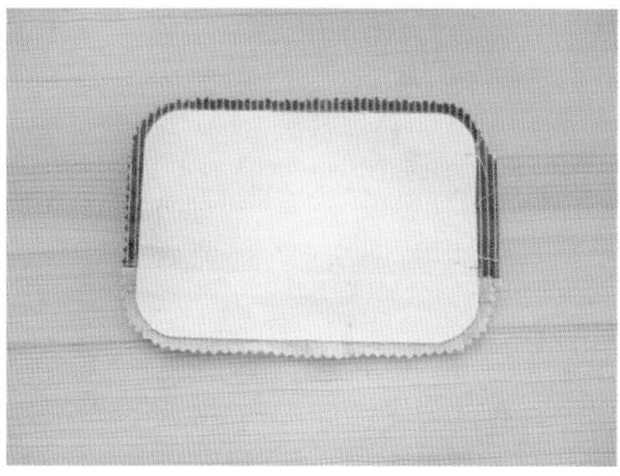

05. Trim the seam allowances along the edges and corners.

06. Turn the pocket right side out and sew the opening closed.

07. The cover of the case is now complete.

08. Attach the leather snap closure, add the plastic wallet insert, and start organizing your cards.

Keepsake Folio

The finished folio measures 11⅞" x 9⅞" x 5⅞" (30 x 25 x 15cm).

Materials:

- ⅓ yd. (⅓m) of light to medium-weight fabric for folio sides and pockets – Fabric A
- ⅓ yd. (⅓m) of light to medium-weight fabric for pockets and patchwork – Fabric B
- ¼ yd. (¼m) of light to medium-weight fabric for patchwork and pencil holder – Fabric C
- ¼ yd. (¼m) of light to medium-weight fabric for various patchwork – Fabric D
- ⅓ yd. (⅓m) of lightweight fabric for lining
- ½ yd. (½m) of 44" (112cm) wide or ⅔ yd. (⅔m) of 22" (56cm) wide heavyweight interfacing
- ¼ yd. (¼m) of 44" (112cm) wide or ½ yd. (½m) of 22" (56cm) wide lightweight interfacing
- 9½" x 4⅜" (24 x 11cm) piece of transparent vinyl
- Two D-rings
- Two magnetic snaps
- Two 8" (20.5cm) zippers
- 9½" (24cm) of wide decorative lace
- 2⅜" (6cm) of cotton ribbon
- Shoulder strap with lobster clasp ends
- 1⅔ yd. (1⅔m) of bias binding tape or fabric to fold your own

Before you begin:

- Use a ⅜" (1cm) seam allowance unless indicated otherwise.
- Note that to get the pattern pieces for the vinyl pocket flap, you will need to trace it from the dotted line of the paper pattern.
- Find and trace the 2 pattern pieces from Side A of the pattern paper. Add seam allowances to the vinyl pocket flap, but not to the main folio body.
- For the inner credit card and flat pockets, iron the interfacing to the outer pocket pieces and not the lining.

Cut the following pieces from your fabric and interfacing:

- **Outer Folio (Flap section):** Constructed in patchwork pieces
  - Piece A – cut a 2⅜" x 4⅜" (6 x 11cm) rectangle: Fabric A (1)
  - Piece B – cut a 3½" x 4⅜" (9 x 11cm) rectangle: Fabric B (1)
  - Piece C – cut a 5⅞" x 5⅛" (15 x 13cm) rectangle: Fabric C (1)
  - Piece D – cut a 9½" x 4¾" (24 x 12cm) rectangle: Fabric D (1)
  - Interfacing – cut a 9½" x 8⅝" (24 x 22cm) rectangle: Heavyweight interfacing (1)
- **Folio Flap Zipper Pocket** – cut an 8⅝" x 9½" (22 x 24cm) rectangle: Lining fabric (1)
- **Zipper Tab** – cut a 2" x 2⅜" (5 x 6cm) rectangle: Fabric A (1)

- **Outer Folio (Body section):** Constructed in patchwork pieces
  - Piece E – cut a 10¼" x 2⅜" (26 x 6cm) rectangle: Fabric A (1)
  - Piece F – cut a 5⅛" x 8⅝" (13 x 24cm) rectangle: Fabric C (1)
  - Piece G – cut a 2¾" x 8⅝" (7 x 24cm) rectangle: Fabric B (1)
  - Piece H – cut a 3⅛" x 8⅝" (8 x 24cm) rectangle: Fabric D (1)
  - Interfacing – cut an 8⅝" x 10⅝" (24 x 27cm) rectangle: Heavyweight interfacing (1)
- **Folio Lining** (from pattern pack): Lining fabric (1), Heavyweight interfacing (1)
- **Vinyl Pocket** – cut a 10⅝" x 4⅜" (24 x 11cm) rectangle: Transparent vinyl (1)
- **Vinyl Binding** – cut a 10⅝" x 1⅛" (24 x 4cm) rectangle: Lining fabric (2)
- **Vinyl Pocket Flap** (from pattern pack): Fabric B (1), Lining fabric (1), Heavyweight interfacing (1)
- **Pencil Holder** – cut a 6⅝" x 2⅜" (17 x 6cm) rectangle: Fabric C (1), Heavyweight interfacing (1)
- **Inner Pockets:**
  - Credit Card Pocket – 7⅞" x 18⅞" cut a (20 x 48cm) rectangle: Fabric B (1)
  - Card Pocket Sides – cut a 1⅛" x 7⅞" (4 x 20cm) rectangle: Fabric A (2)
  - Flat Pocket – cut a 10⅝" x 10⅝" (24 x 24cm) square: Fabric B (1), Fabric A (1)
  - Center Zipper Pocket – cut an 8⅝" x 11⅞" (22 x 30cm) rectangle: Fabric B (1), Lining fabric (1), Lightweight interfacing (1)
- **Folio Sides** – cut a 12⅝" x 5⅛" (32 x 13cm) rectangle: Fabric A (2), Lightweight interfacing (2)

Instructions

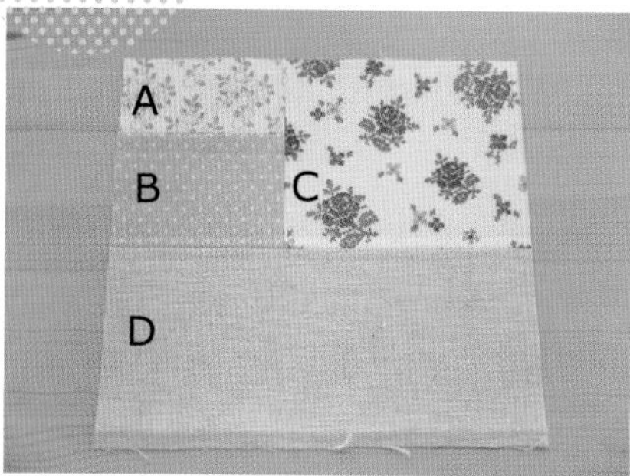

01. Sew together the various patchwork pieces as indicated in the photograph to create the outer folio flap. When finished, iron the interfacing onto the back, then apply the decorative lace along the seam connecting piece D.

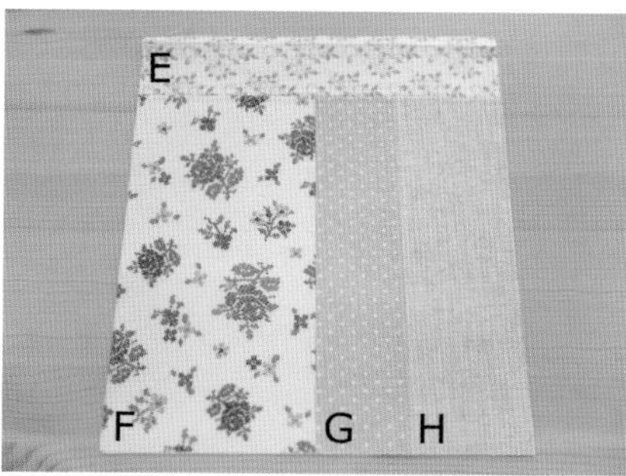

02. Repeat the same instructions for the patchwork pieces for the outer folio body, then iron the interfacing as before.

03. Create the zipper tab for the beginning end of the zipper. Fold under the short edges by ⅜" (1cm), then fold the whole tab in half with wrong sides together. Fold the tab over the beginning of the zipper, then edge stitch the folds in place. To install the zipper, begin by folding under the short edge of the outer folio flap by ⅜" (1cm) and layering it over the zipper tape. Layer the flap zipper pocket piece beneath it with the right side facing up and edge stitch along the fold of the outer fabric to sew all three layers in place.

04. Fold the bottom edge of the flap pocket fabric upward, effectively folding the fabric in half to align with the remaining edge of the zipper tape. Follow the previous instructions to apply the outer folio body to the other side of the zipper, resulting in the flap zipper pocket. The finished fabric piece should measure 9½" x 19⅝" (24 x 50cm).

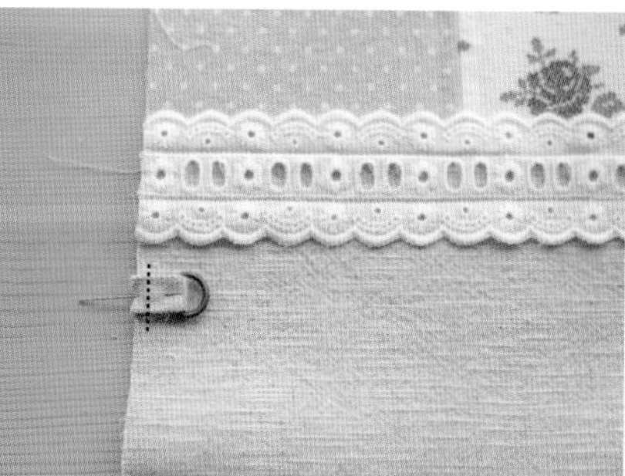

05. Take the cotton ribbon and cut two 1⅛" (3cm) pieces. Loop them through the D-rings and baste them along each side of the outer folio, above the lace from step 1.

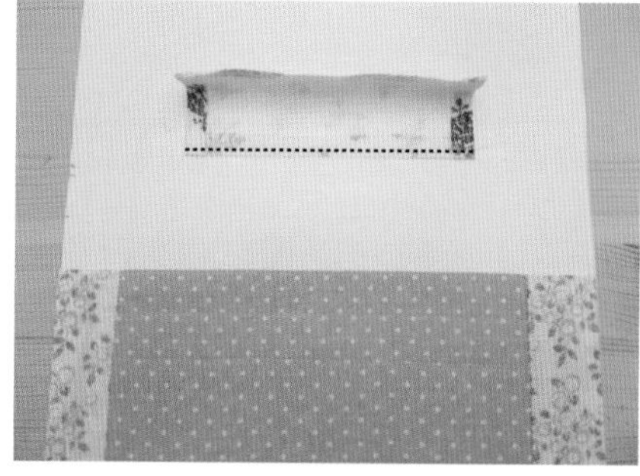

06. Trim the interfacing for the pencil holder to 5⅛" x 1½" (13 x 4cm) and iron it to the fabric. Fold under the short edges by ⅜" (1cm) and baste them in place. Iron the interfacing to the folio lining, then line up the long raw edge of the pencil holder against the pattern guideline on the folio lining. Sew it in place 1⁄16" (0.2cm) from the edge.

07. Fold the pencil holder in half with wrong sides together, matching up the long edges; then sew the layers in place ¼" (0.5cm) from the edge.

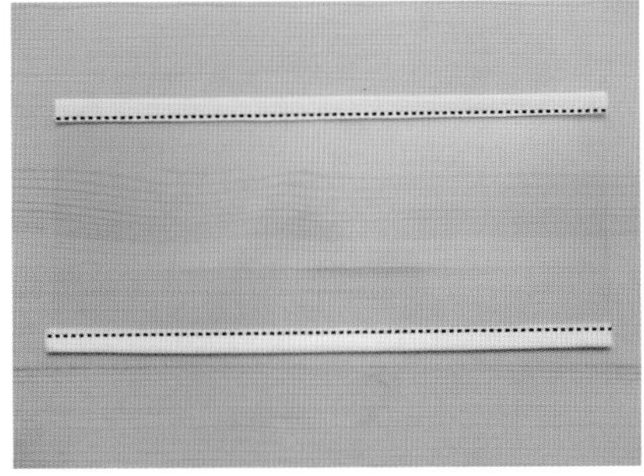

08. Using the vinyl binding fabric, bind the long edges of the vinyl pocket following the instructions in Essential Techniques K (pg. 122).

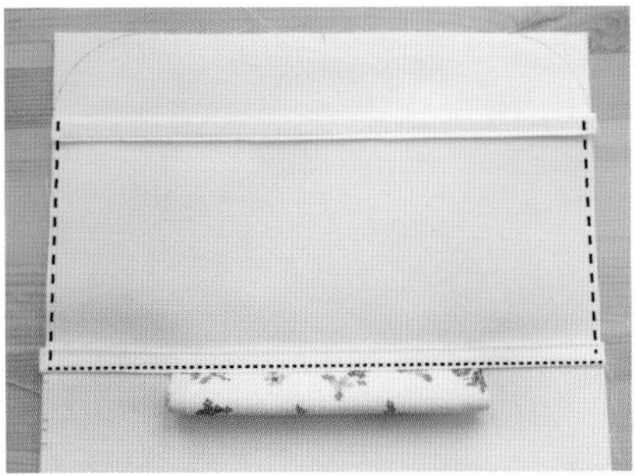

09. Line up the bottom edge of the vinyl pocket where the pattern guidelines indicate on the folio lining, then baste the sides in place and edge stitch the bottom edge of the pocket in place.

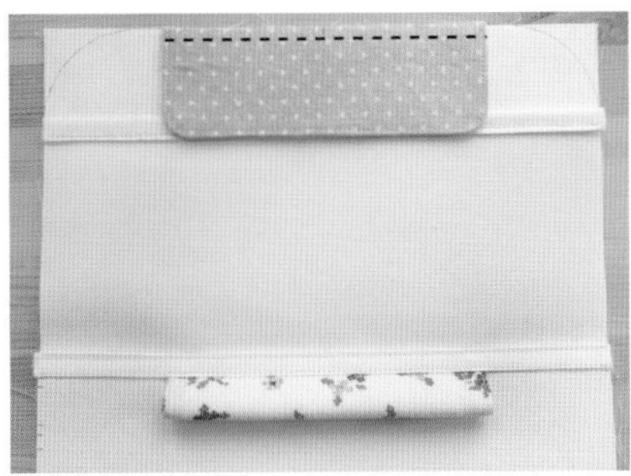

10. Create the folio flap following the instructions in Essential Techniques B: Version 1 (pg. 108). Then sew it to the folio lining according to the pattern guidelines.

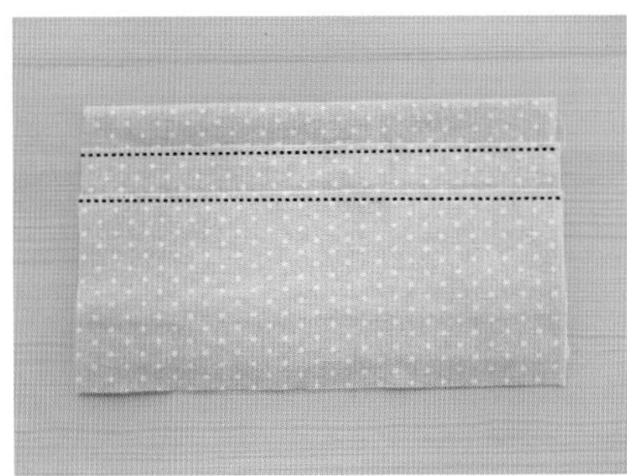

11. To create the credit card pocket, take the pocket fabric and make horizontal marks going up the length of the fabric at 3⅛", 6¼", 10¼", 13⅜", and 16½" (8, 16, 26, 34, and 42cm). Treat these marks as accordion folds, folding over at 3⅛" (8cm), under at 6¼" (16cm) and so on in that manner to create the shape seen in the photograph. Iron the folds, then edge stitch along the first two over folds.

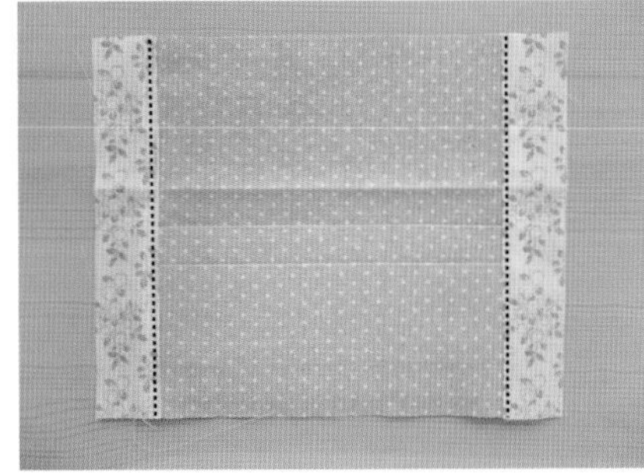

12. Unfold the last fold in your accordion upwards, and the side edges should match up with the card pocket side pieces. Sew them together along the side edges, resulting in the card pocket in the middle and side panels on the sides. Iron the seam allowances toward the side panels, then edge stitch the seams.

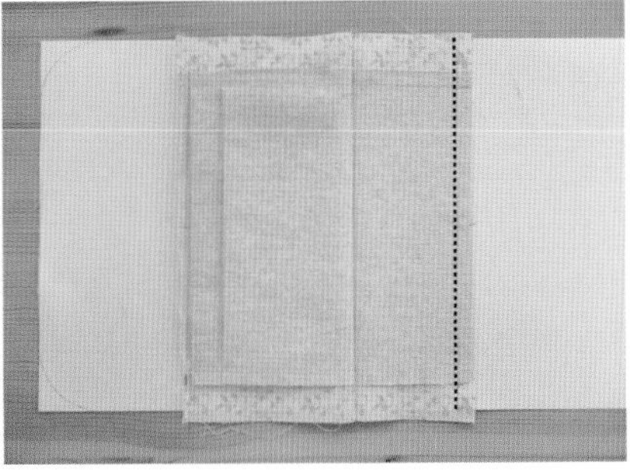

13. Fold the top fold back down (along with the side panel fabric) as it was in step 11 and iron the fold in place. With wrong sides together, layer the card pocket over the folio lining where the guidelines indicate, aligning the top edge where the pattern shows. While holding onto the top fold, flip back the bottom folds, revealing the fold you made at 13⅜" (34cm). Sew this fold to the folio lining ⅜" (1cm) away from the edge.

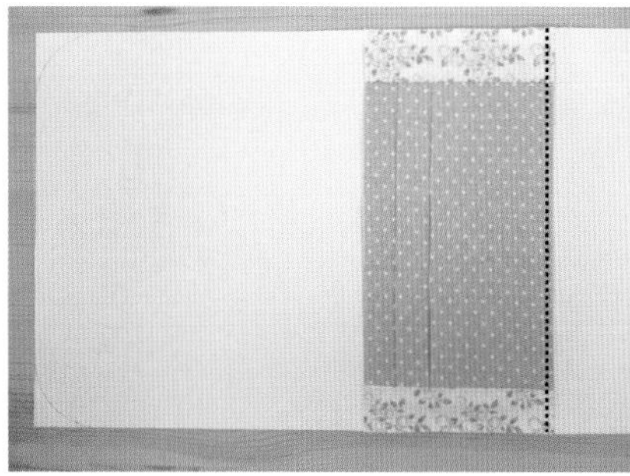

14. Flip the folds back to where they were previously, then fold under the bottom edge of the pocket by ⅜" (1cm). The bottom edge of the pocket should now match up with the pattern guideline. Edge stitch the fold in place to secure the bottom of the pocket to the folio lining.

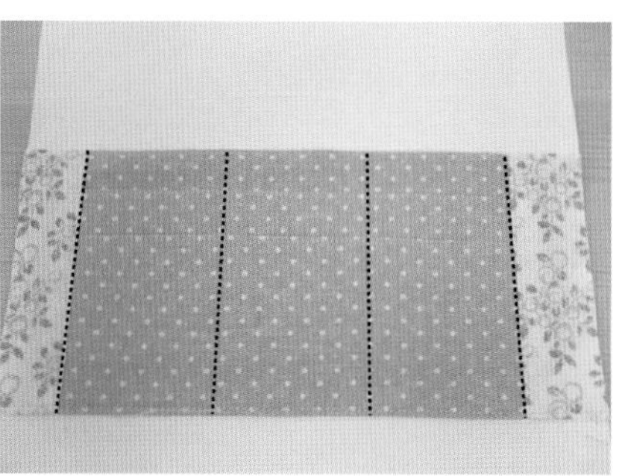

15. Sew vertical seams at 2⅝" (6.5cm) and 5¼" (13.5cm) out from the side panels to create separations for the credit card pockets. This finishes the credit card pocket.

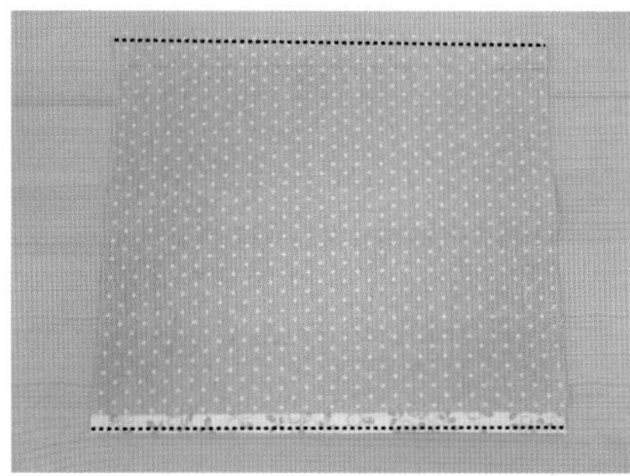

16. For the flat pocket, sew the outer and lining pieces together along the short sides with right sides facing. Turn the fabric right side out, and shift the seams at the end so the fabric folds against the seam allowances, causing a ⅜" (1cm) strip of the opposing fabric to show on each side. Edge stitch along each fold.

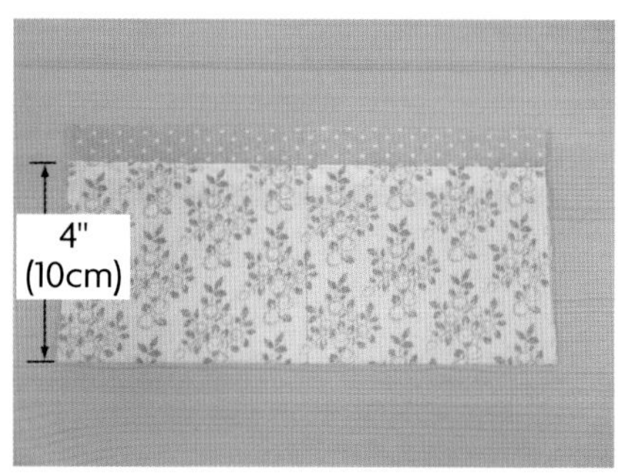

17. Fold the bottom edge upward by 4" (10cm) and iron the fold in place.

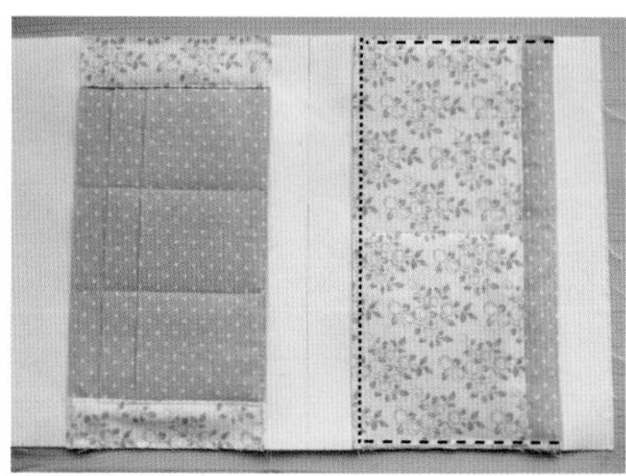

18. Line up the newly folded edge of the pocket where the guidelines on the pattern indicate, pointing the top of the pocket towards the bottom of the folio lining. Baste the pocket in place along the sides, then edge stitch it along the bottom fold.

19. For the folio sides, iron the interfacing to the wrong side of the fabric, then fold them in half widthwise and sew them together along the short edge. Turn the fabric right side out and iron it flat. Edge stitch along both 5⅛" (13cm) edges, then iron it in half widthwise.

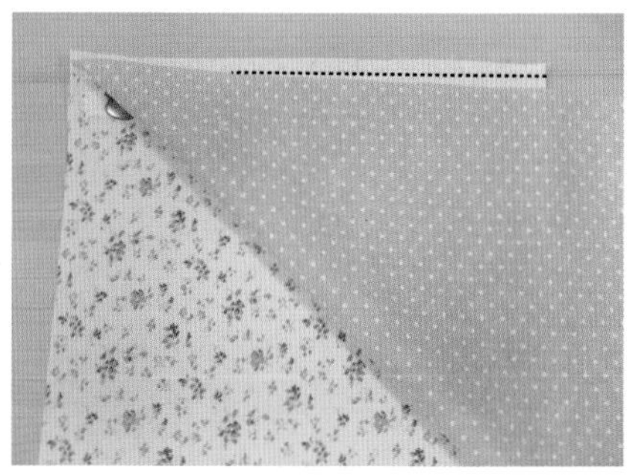

20. For the center zipper pocket, iron the interfacing to what will be the outer pocket fabric, then layer the zipper between the short edges of the pocket fabric and lining with right sides together. Sew the three layers together along the edge.

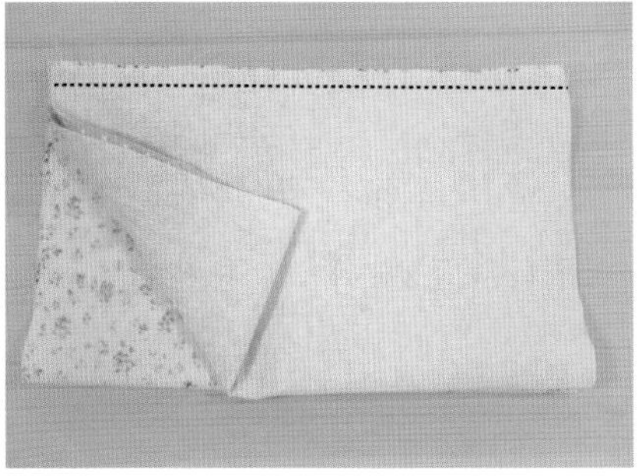

21. Bring up the opposite ends of the pocket fabric and sew them to the remaining edge of the zipper tape as in the previous step. The sides should be left unsewn.

22. Turn the fabric right side out and tuck the lining into the outer pocket fabric. Baste the sides of the pocket.

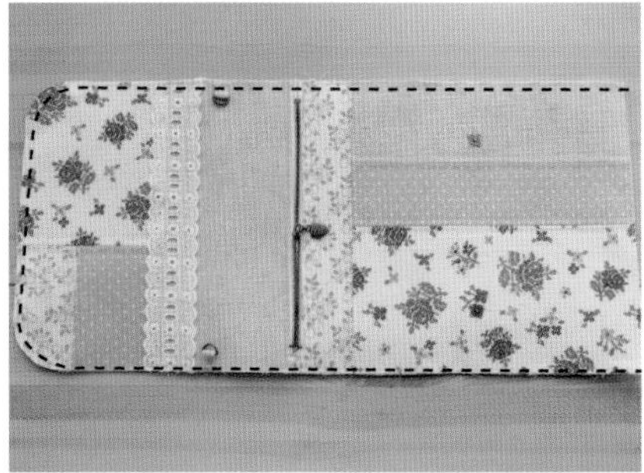

23. Install the magnetic snaps where the pattern indicates on the outer folio and lining. Then layer the outer folio and lining sections together with wrong sides facing. Trim the top end of the outer folio according to the pattern so the fabric has rounded corners, then baste all the layers together.

24. Line up the folio side pieces near the middle third of the inner folio (have the fold creases from step 19 pointing inward), with the bottom edge lined up where the pattern indicates. Baste the side edges in place, then wrap the bottom third of the folio upward to line up the remaining folio side where the other pattern guideline indicates. Align the edge of the folio side as before and baste it in place as the photograph shows. When the folio sides are completely sewn in place, refer to Essential Techniques K (pg. 122) to wrap the entire edge of the folio body with bias binding.

25. Pull the folio sides outward, folded in half, then tuck the raw edges of the zipper pocket within the fold. Sew a seam here to anchor one side of the pocket in place. Repeat with the other folio side to complete the pocket.

26. Attach the strap to the D-rings, and your keepsake folio is ready for memories.

Slippers

Materials:

- ¼ yd. (¼m) of medium-weight fabric for instep
- ⅓ yd. (⅓m) of lightweight fabric for lining
- ⅓ yd. (⅓m) of 44" (112cm) wide or ⅔ yd. (⅔m) of 22" (56cm) wide heavyweight interfacing
- ¼ yd. (¼m) of non-skid gripping fabric for sole of slipper
- Pair of shoe insoles
- 11" (28cm) of wide decorative lace

Before you begin:

- Use a ⅜" (1cm) seam allowance unless indicated otherwise.
- Find and trace the 2 pattern pieces from Side A of the pattern paper, remembering to add ⅜" (1cm) seam allowances.
- Note that the shoe insoles serve to both cushion your feet and extend the life and comfort of your slippers no matter where you wear them. If the insoles are too large, you can trim them until they fit the size of the slippers.

Cut the following pieces from your fabric and interfacing:

- **Instep** (from pattern pack): Main outer fabric (2), Lining fabric (2), Heavyweight interfacing (4)
- **Sole** (from pattern pack): Non-slip fabric (2), Lining fabric (2), Heavyweight interfacing (2)

Instructions

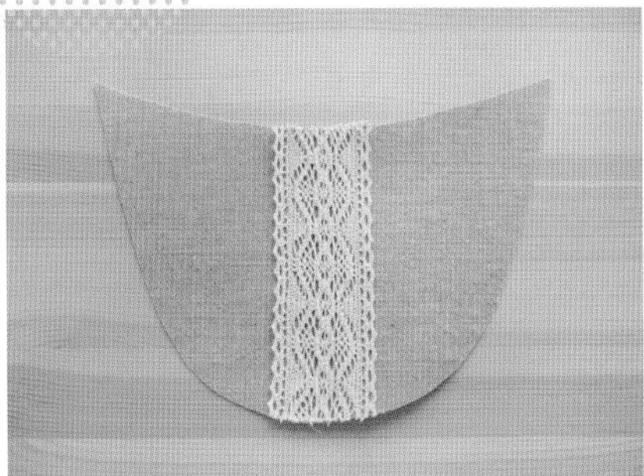

01. For the instep, iron the interfacing to the main fabric and lining pieces. Then sew the decorative lace vertically across the outer fabric.

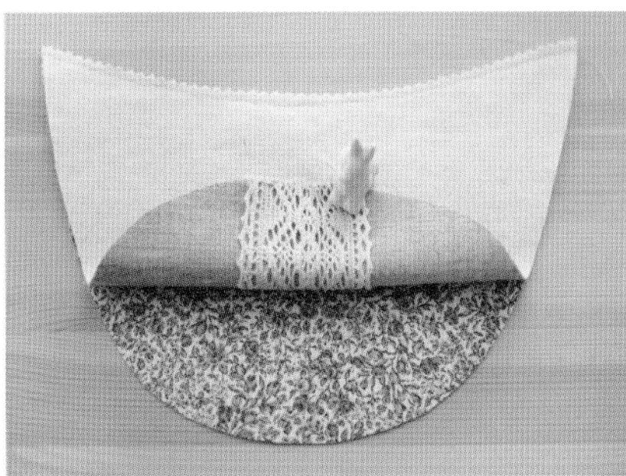

02. Layer the outer fabric of the instep with the lining, right sides together. Sew them along the inner curved edge of the shape, along the top side. Trim the seam allowances and iron the seam.

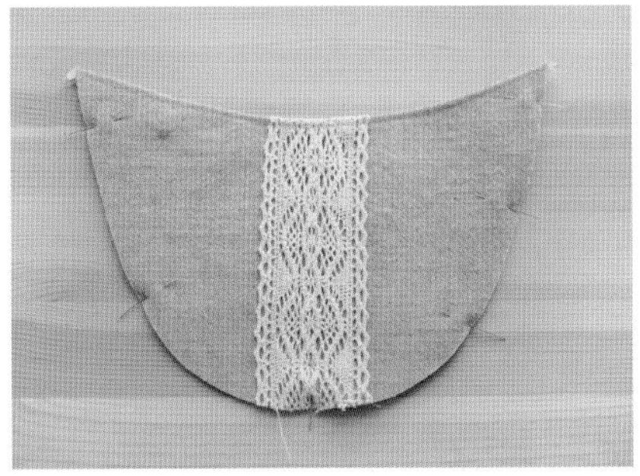

03. Turn the fabric right side out and secure the two layers together with pins around the raw edges.

04. Line up the instep fabric along the non-slip fabric with right sides together. Beginning at the head of the slipper, align the edges and pin in place, going outward around the sole and following the pattern markings.

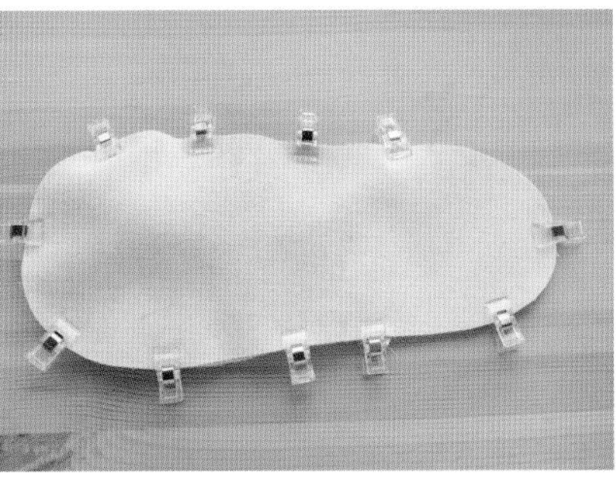

05. Layer the sole lining fabric over the non-slip fabric with right sides facing, and match up the raw edges, clipping them in place.

06. Sew a seam around the perimeter of the sole, leaving an opening at the head of the slipper where the pattern indicates.

07. Turn the slipper right side out, then slip the insole inside. Sew the opening shut with a slip stitch.

08. That completes one slipper; follow the same steps to complete your pair.

Slipper Bag

Materials:

- ¼ yd. (¼m) of medium-weight fabric for main bag
- 8" (20.5cm) of wide eyelet lace
- 15¾" (40cm) of wide lace for drawstring casing
- 17" (43cm) of suede cording for drawstring
- Small decorative metal medallion

Before you begin:

- Use a ⅜" (1cm) seam allowance unless indicated otherwise.

Cut the following pieces from your fabric:

- **Bag Body** – cut a 7⅞" x 28⅜" (20 x 72cm) rectangle: Main outer fabric (1)

01. Fold the bag body in half widthwise to find the center point. Apply the decorative lace about 1" (2.5cm) up from this line, sew on the decorative metal medallion, then fold the bag in half again. Tuck in the center fold by ⅝" (1.5cm) and baste these folds in place for the bottom of the bag.

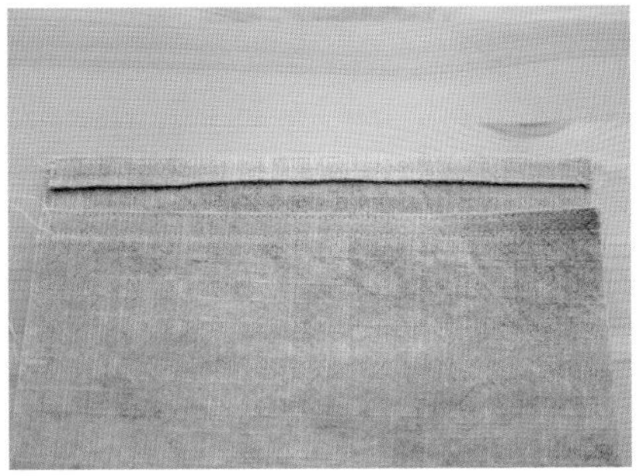

02. Make a double-fold hem along the short edges of the bag body by folding over ⅜" (1cm) twice and sewing the folds in place. This creates the opening edge of the bag.

03. Cut the drawstring casing lace in two, then fold over the raw ends and sew them in place.

04. Line up the drawstring casing lace pieces ¾" (2cm) below the top edges of the bag. Sew them in place along the top and bottom edges.

05. Fold the bag in half with wrong sides together and sew along the two sides with ¼" (0.5cm) seam allowances.

06. Turn the bag inside out and press the previous seams flat. Then sew the side seams again with a ⅜" (1cm) seam allowance, creating a French seam.

07. Turn the bag right side out again and thread the suede cording through the drawstring casing lace. You are now ready to take your slippers on the go.

Water Bottle Sleeve

The finished water bottle case measures 3⅛" x 3⅛" x 9⅞" (8 x 8 x 25cm).

Materials:

- ⅛ yd. (⅛m) of complementing light to medium-weight fabric for upper case
- ¼ yd. (¼m) of light to medium-weight fabric for main case
- ¼ yd. (¼m) of lightweight fabric for lining
- 4" x 4" (10 x 10cm) scrap of heavyweight interfacing
- 12" (30.5cm) of narrow decorative lace
- Small lace medallion

Before you begin:

- Use a ⅜" (1cm) seam allowance unless indicated otherwise.
- Find and trace the 3 pattern pieces from Side B of the pattern paper, remembering to add ⅜" (1cm) seam allowances.

Cut the following pieces from your fabric:

- **Upper Sleeve** (from pattern pack): Contrast fabric (2)
- **Lower Sleeve** (from pattern pack): Main outer fabric (2)
- **Sleeve Lining** – cut a 5¾" x 10⅝" (14.5 x 27cm) rectangle: Lining fabric (2)
- **Sleeve Bottom** (from pattern pack): Main outer fabric (1), Lining fabric (1), Heavyweight interfacing (1)
- **Drawstring** – cut a 1½" x 28¾" (4 x 73cm) rectangle: Main outer fabric (1)

Instructions

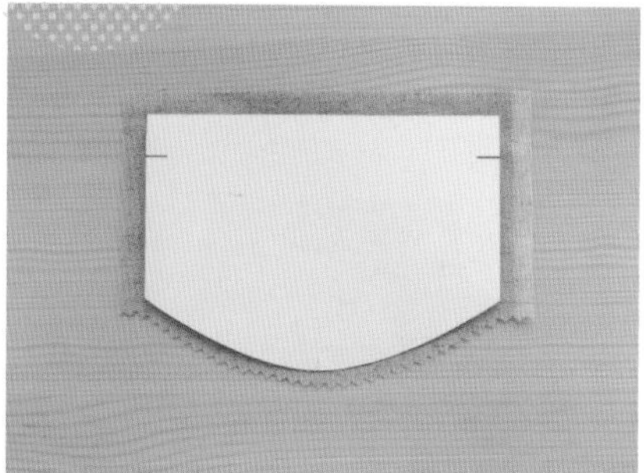

01. Sew a zigzag stitch along the bottom edge of the upper sleeve. Repeat this with the other upper sleeve piece.

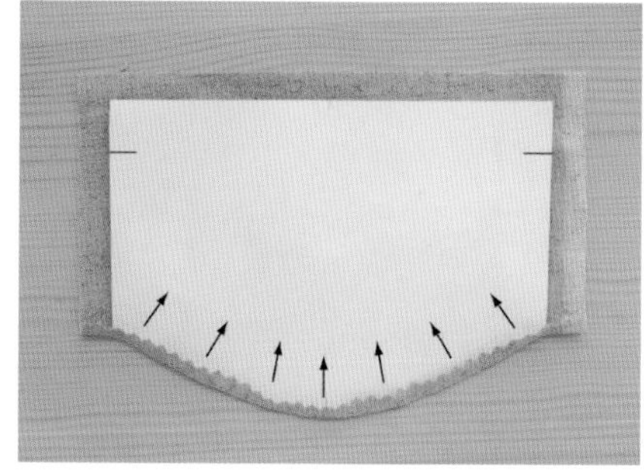

02. Using the paper pattern without seam allowances as a guide, line up the paper over the center of the upper sleeve and fold up the bottom edge against the paper. Iron the folds in place very firmly to keep the shape.

03. Layer the edge of the upper sleeve over the top edge of the lower sleeve, right sides facing up. Then edge stitch the upper sleeve in place along the fold. Apply the decorative lace along the seam and the lace medallion in the middle.

04. Layer the outer sleeve with the lining, right sides facing together, and sew them together along the upper edge. Repeat this with the remaining outer sleeve and lining pieces.

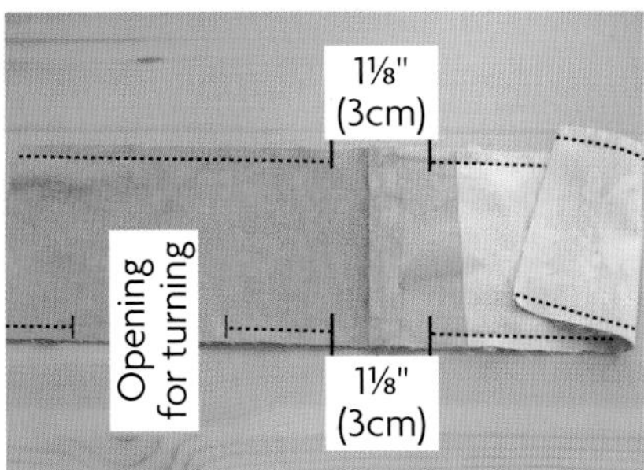

05. Unfold the fabric pieces, and layer them together with the lining facing the lining and outer fabric facing the outer fabric, right sides together. Sew around the perimeter of the fabric, except for a 1⅛" (3cm) space centered along the top seams, and another opening along the side of the lining for turning the sleeve right side out.

06. Iron the interfacing to the sleeve bottom outer fabric. Sew the bottom edge of the outer sleeve around the perimeter of the sleeve bottom. Repeat this with the lining pieces as well.

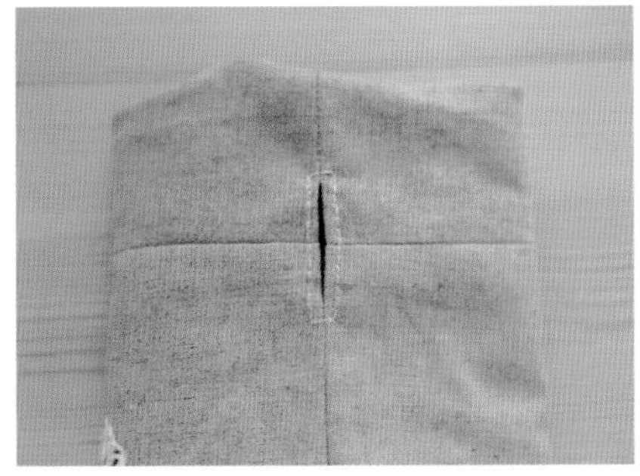

07. Turn the sleeve right side out from the opening in the lining, then sew the opening closed. For the openings in the top edge of the sleeve, hand sew a backstitch going around the perimeter of the opening.

08. Sew a seam around the top edge of the bag ¾" (2cm) down from the top seam.

09. For the drawstring, fold under the long edges by ⅜" (1cm) and iron the folds. Then fold over the whole strap lengthwise with wrong sides together and edge stitch along both edges of the strap.

10. Thread the drawstring through the casing at the top of the sleeve, then tie a knot on one end to secure it. Your bottle sleeve is complete.

Towel Clip

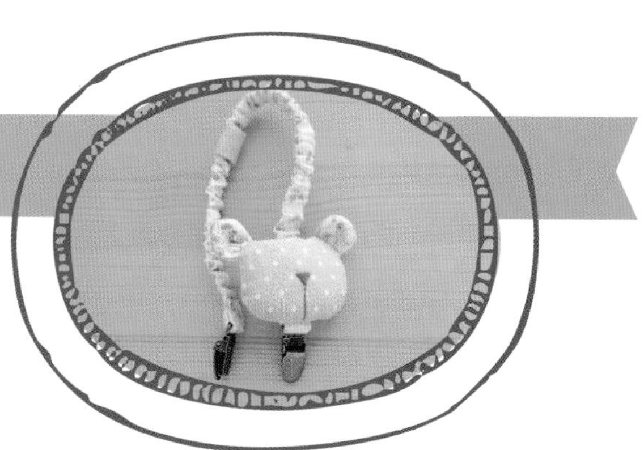

The finished towel clip measures 2⅜" x 11⅞" (6 x 30cm).

Materials:

- 7" x 5" (18 x 12.5cm) scrap of lightweight fabric for bear head
- 13" x 4" (33 x 10cm) scrap of lightweight complementing fabric for elastic strap
- Two name badge clips
- 11⅞" (30cm) of ½" (1.5cm) wide elastic
- Batting
- Embroidery floss

Before you begin:

- Use a ⅜" (1cm) seam allowance unless indicated otherwise.
- Find and trace the 2 pattern pieces from Side A of the pattern paper, remembering to add ⅜" (1cm) seam allowances.

Cut the following pieces from your fabric:

- **Bear Head** (from pattern pack): Main fabric (2)
- **Bear Ears** (from pattern pack): Main fabric (2), Contrasting fabric (2)
- **Elastic Strip** – cut a 12¼" x 1⅛" (31 x 4cm) rectangle: Contrasting fabric (1)

Instructions

01. Take the ear outer and inner fabric and line them together with right sides facing. Sew them together along the rounded edge, clip the seam allowances, then turn the ear right side out through the opening along the straight edge. Repeat for the second ear.

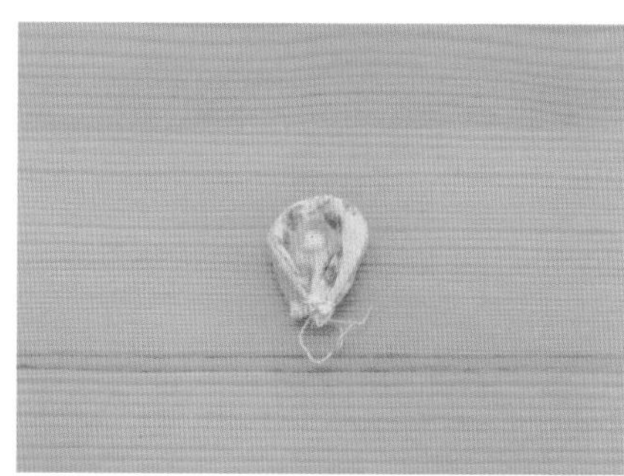

02. Using a little hand gathering stitch, cinch up the bottom edge of the bear ear and tie a sturdy knot.

03. Transfer the placement marks from the pattern onto the wrong side of the bear head fabric. Line up the bear ears with the placement marks, then sandwich the ears between the two pieces of head fabric with right sides of the head fabric facing.

04. Sew around the entire edge of the bear head.

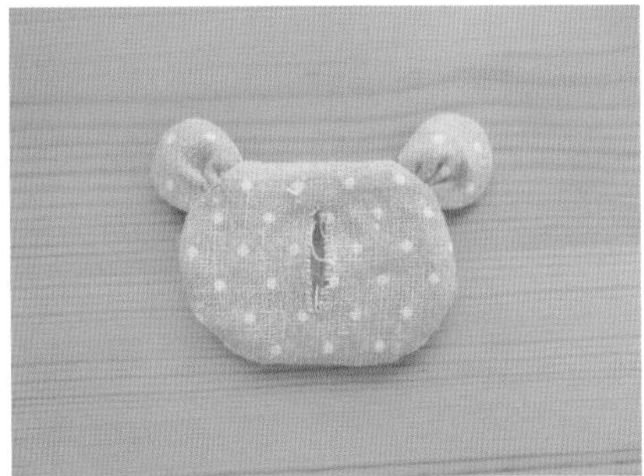

05. Cut a small opening on the back side of the bear head and turn the head right side out.

06. Stuff the head with batting and sew the opening closed. Then embroider the nose and mouth onto the front of the bear head. Alternatively, you could embroider the nose and mouth before step 3.

07. Fold the strip fabric in half lengthwise with right sides together. Sew along the long edge of the strip, using a ¼" (0.5cm) seam allowance, making it into a tube.

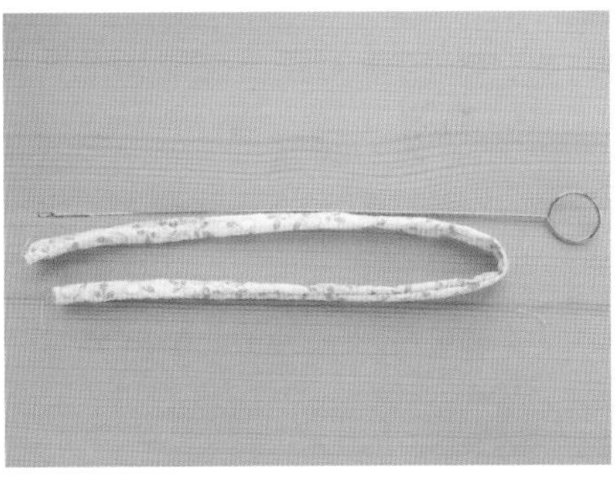

08. Use a loop turner to turn the fabric right side out.

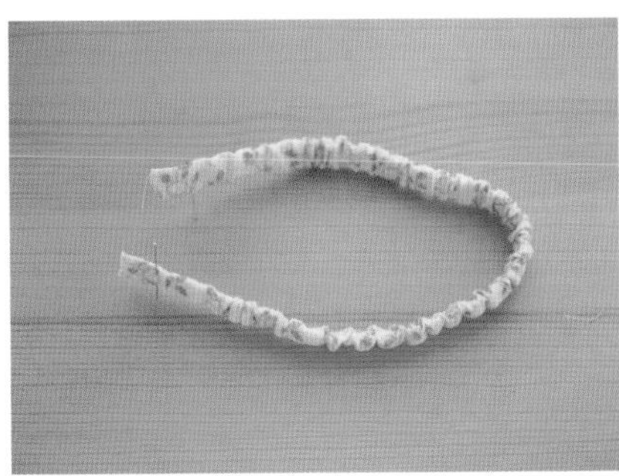

09. Use a bodkin to pull the elastic through the fabric. Center the elastic in the middle, leaving fabric extending ¼" (0.5cm) from each end.

10. Attach the badge clips to both ends by folding the extra fabric over and securing it with a box stitch. Be sure to stitch through the elastic at both ends as well, to hold it in place.

11. Sew the bear head in place on the elastic strap. You have finished your towel clip.

Bucket Hat

The finished hat measures 22" (56cm) for a medium and 23¼" (59cm) for a large.

Materials:

- ¼ yd. (¼m) medium-weight fabric for main hat
- ¼ yd. (¼m) of complementing medium-weight fabric for contrast panel
- ¼ yd. (¼m) of lightweight fabric for lining
- ¼ yd. (¼m) of 44" (112cm) or ⅔ yd. (⅔m) of 22" (56cm) wide heavyweight interfacing
- 6" (15cm) of narrow decorative lace
- Small decorative lace medallion

Before you begin:

- Use a ⅜" (1cm) seam allowance unless indicated otherwise.
- Find and trace the 4 pattern pieces from Side B of the pattern paper, remembering to add ⅜" (1cm) seam allowances.
- Note that if you prefer the hat to be more soft and pliable, you don't have to use interfacing.

Cut the following pieces from your fabric and interfacing:

Note that the interfacing is cut without seam allowances to reduce bulk.

- **Brim** (from pattern pack): Main outer fabric (5), Heavyweight interfacing (5), Lining fabric (6)
- **Upper Front Panel** (from pattern pack): Contrast fabric (1), Heavyweight interfacing (1)
- **Lower Front Panel** (from pattern pack): Main outer fabric (1), Heavyweight interfacing (1)
- **Crown** (from pattern pack): Main outer fabric (1), Lining fabric (1), Heavyweight interfacing (1)

Instructions

01. Gather together and prepare your hat brim lining pieces. Apply the interfacing to the outer fabric hat pieces.

02. Take two of the brim pieces and line them up with right sides together. Sew a seam along one side, then press the seam open.

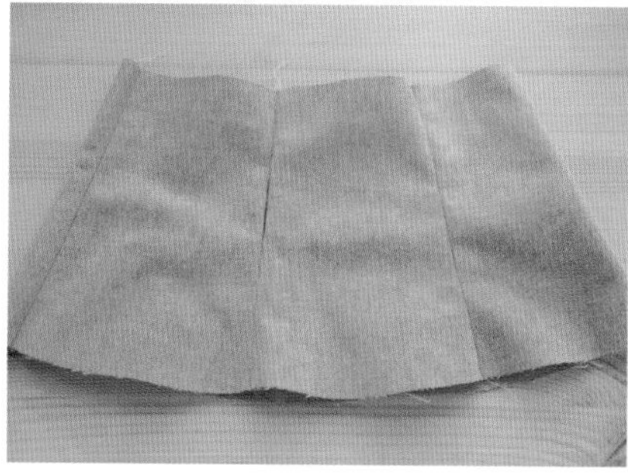

03. Repeat this process with the rest of the brim lining pieces, sewing them all in a row. Connect the end pieces to create a ring, but leave an opening in the seam for turning the hat right side out later.

04. Line up the top edge of the hat brim around the perimeter of the hat crown. The seams from the brim pieces should match up with the markings on the pattern. Stitch the hat crown in place. When finished, iron the seam allowances in the direction of the crown.

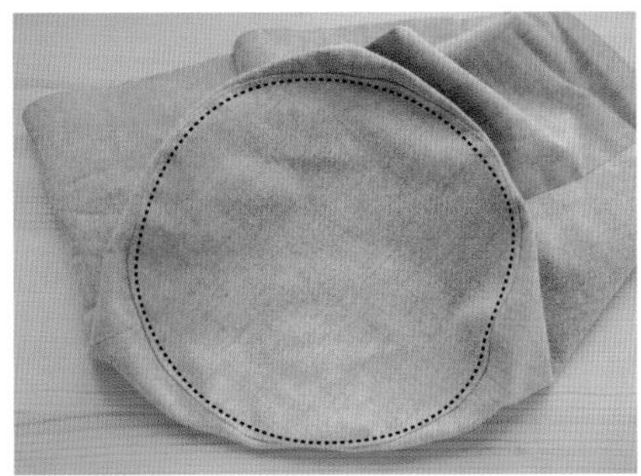

05. Edge stitch the seam allowances around the perimeter of the crown. This completes the lining for the hat.

06. Sew the upper front panel to the lower front panel. Apply the decorative lace along the seam and the small lace medallion in the middle.

07. Repeat the instructions for step 2 with the outer hat brim pieces. When the side seam is sewn, edge stitch the seam on each side.

08. Continue onward as in step 3, still edge stitching the seam allowances as you go. Do not leave an opening in the last seam, unlike the lining pieces.

09. Repeat the instructions for steps 4 and 5 with the outer brim pieces to attach the crown.

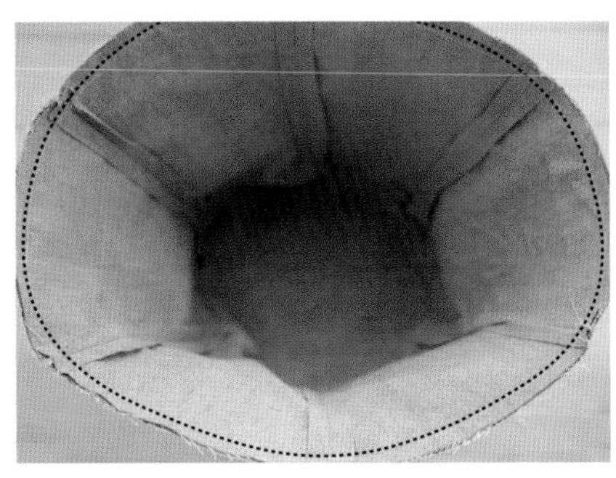

10. Place the outer hat and lining together with right sides facing and sew a seam along the bottom edge.

11. Press the seam open, then trim the seam allowances with pinking shears.

12. Turn the hat right side out and iron it completely. Sew the opening in the lining closed, then edge stitch the bottom edge to complete your bucket hat.

Baby's Bib

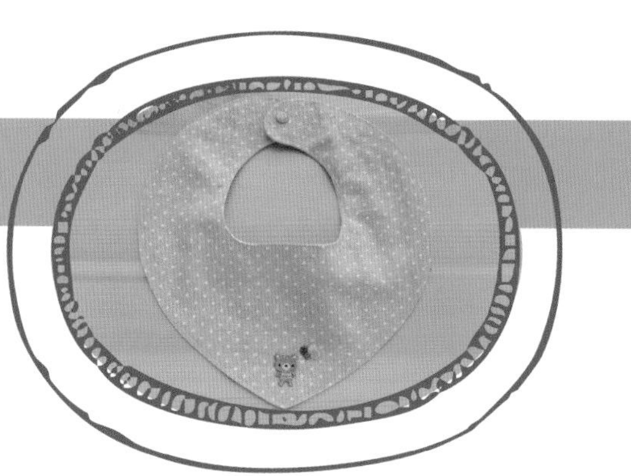

The finished round bib measures 8⅝" x 13" (22 x 33cm), while the triangular bib measures 9½" x 9⅞" (24 x 25cm).

Materials:

FOR ROUND BIB:

- ¼ yd. (¼m) of lightweight fabric for outer patchwork – Fabric A
- ⅛ yd. (⅛m) of lightweight fabric for outer patchwork – Fabric B
- ⅛ yd. (⅛m) of lightweight fabric for outer patchwork – Fabric C
- ⅓ yd. (⅓m) of lightweight fabric for lining
- ⅓ yd. (⅓m) of lightweight interfacing
- Snap button

FOR TRIANGULAR BIB:

- ⅓ yd. (⅓m) of lightweight fabric for outer bib
- ⅓ yd. (⅓m) of lightweight fabric for lining
- ⅓ yd. (⅓m) of lightweight interfacing
- Snap button
- Iron-on embroidered appliqué patch

Before you begin:

- Use a ⅜" (1cm) seam allowance unless indicated otherwise.
- Find and trace the 2 pattern pieces from Side B of the pattern paper, remembering to add ⅜" (1cm) seam allowances.

Cut the following pieces from your fabric:

- **Round Bib:**
  - Outer Fabric – Assembled from patchwork pieces:
    - Block A – cut a 5⅞" x 13¾" (15 x 35cm) rectangle: Fabric A (1)
    - Block B – cut a 3⅛" x 2¾" (8 x 7cm) rectangle: Fabric B (1)
    - Block C – cut a 4⅜" x 6⅜" (11 x 16cm) rectangle: Fabric B (1)
    - Block D – cut a 4⅜" x 4" (11 x 10cm) rectangle: Fabric C (1)
  - Lining (from pattern pack): Lining fabric (1), Lightweight interfacing (1)
- **Triangular Bib:**
  - Bib Body (from pattern pack): Outer fabric (1), Lining fabric (1), Lightweight interfacing (1)

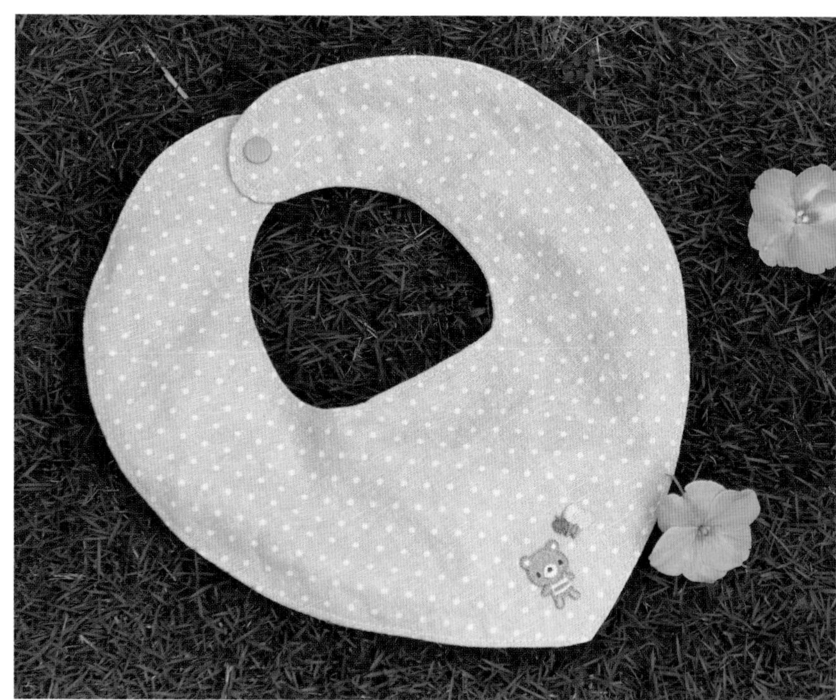

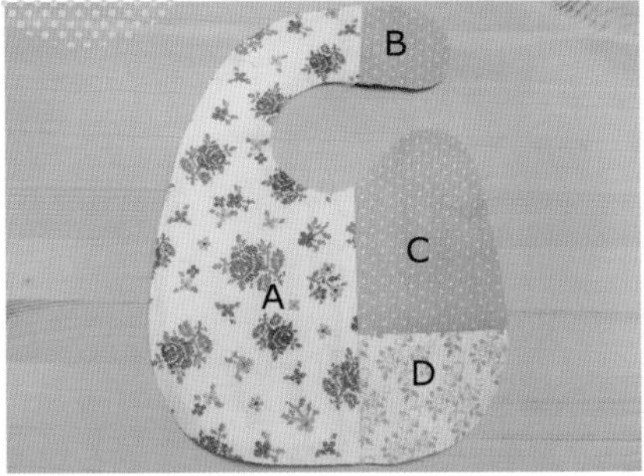

01. For the round bib, assemble the patchwork pieces as seen in the photograph. Sew the C block to the D block along the 4⅜" (11cm) edge, then sew that block along the bottom side of block A. Sew block B against the upper edge. Use the paper pattern to trace the fabric to the correct shape and iron the interfacing, adding an extra layer or two for where the snap will be installed.

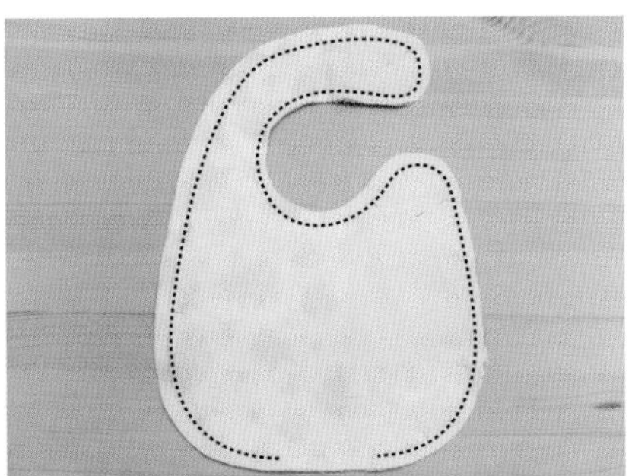

02. Layer the outer fabric and the lining with right sides together and sew around the entire perimeter of the fabric, making sure to leave a 2¾" (7cm) opening along the bottom of the bib. Iron the seam flat.

03. Turn the bib right side out from the opening and iron the whole front side of the bib.

04. Edge stitch around the entire perimeter of the bib.

05. Attach the snap at the tab and upper corner, and you have completed your round baby bib.

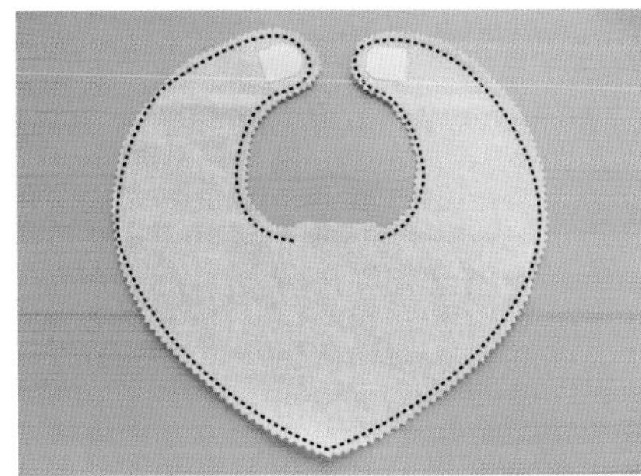

06. For the triangular bib, iron the interfacing to the outer fabric, then place the outer and lining fabric together with front sides facing. Sew them together around the raw edges, leaving a 2" (5cm) opening along the top center edge.

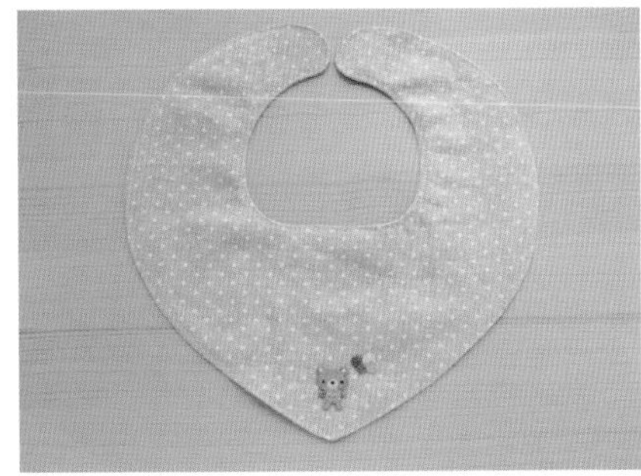

07. Turn the bib right side out and iron it flat. Edge stitch around the entire edge of the bib, and iron on the embroidery appliqué.

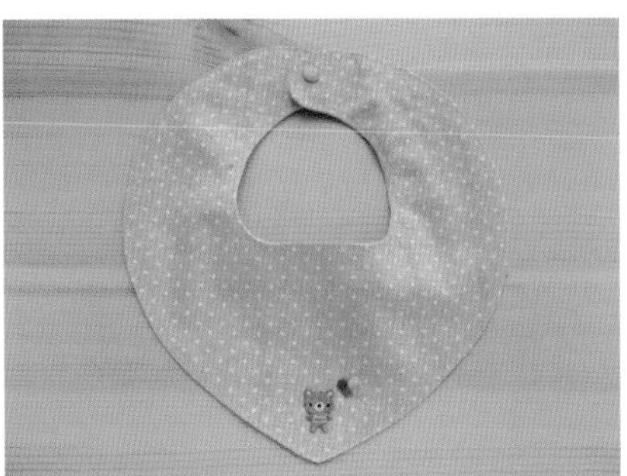

08. Attach the snap button at the tabs, and you have completed the triangular bib.

Essential Techniques

A Quick Guide to Useful Sewing Tricks

A. Three-Dimensional Bag Flaps

B. Flat Bag Flaps

C. Compartment Pockets

D. Three-Dimensional Pockets

E. Elastic Pockets

F. Zipper Pockets

G. Purse Feet

H. Wrist Straps

I. Shoulder Straps

J. Leather-Bordered Labels

K. Bias Binding

L. Piping

M. Magnetic Snaps and Push-Lock Clasps

A: Three-Dimensional Bag Flaps

Before you begin:

- If you use a fabric like cotton burlap, only a single layer of interfacing is needed for the outer fabric, as any more would create too much bulk.
- If you attach a push-lock style clasp to the flap, you'll need to apply an extra layer of interfacing to the lining fabric to reinforce it. Attach the clasp before sewing the flap to the bag body.

Version 1: Single Layer Flap: 2 pieces of fabric (outer fabric and lining)

01. When cutting the flap pieces, it is not necessary to add a seam allowance to the top edge of the outer fabric. Add a ¼" (0.5cm) seam allowance to the top edge of the lining fabric. You can roughly cut the fabric first, iron the interfacing, sew the seam, and then trim it afterwards.

02. Place the outer fabric and lining pieces together with right sides facing. Sew a seam along the side and bottom edges to anchor them in place. Trim the seam allowances along the rounded edges.

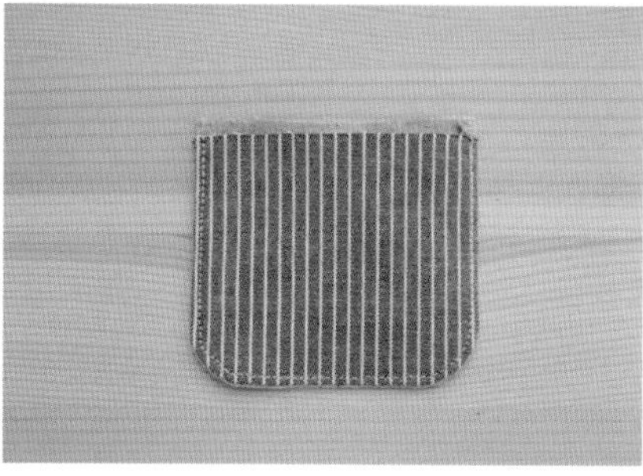

03. Turn the flap right side out and iron it. Edge stitch around the side and bottom edges to secure the edges together. You'll see that the lining fabric extends slightly beyond the outer fabric.

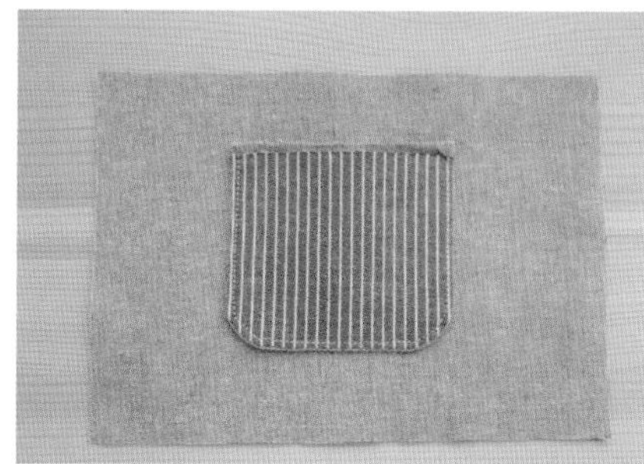

04. Place the flap on the main fabric of the bag with the right sides both facing up. Sew a seam just outside the edge of the outer fabric.

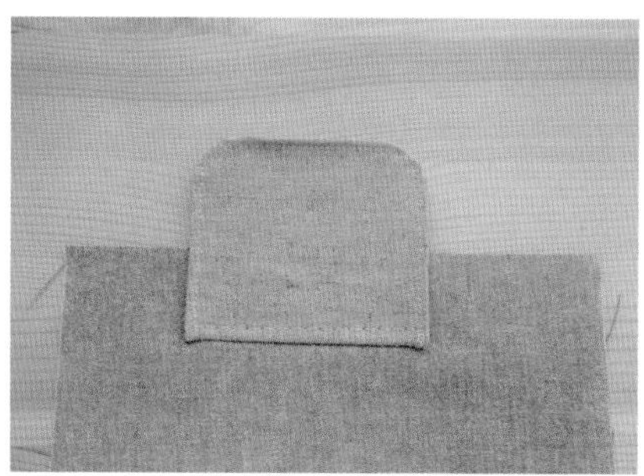

05. Lift the flap up and with a seam allowance of 5⁄16" (0.7cm), sew a seam to secure the flap.

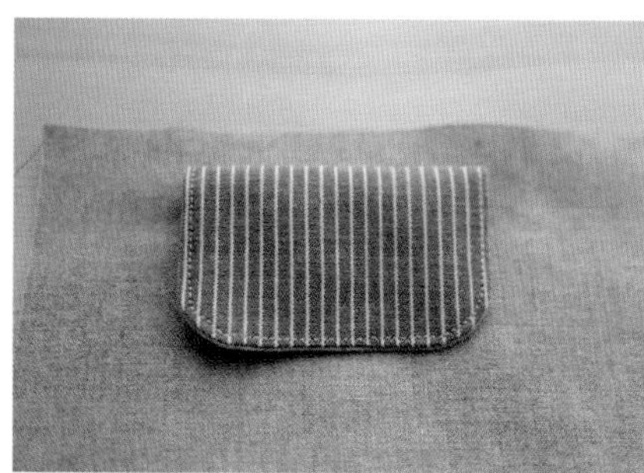

06. You have finished your bag flap.

Version 2: Double-Layered Flap: 4 pieces of fabric (outer fabric and lining for the top layer, outer fabric and lining for the bottom layer)

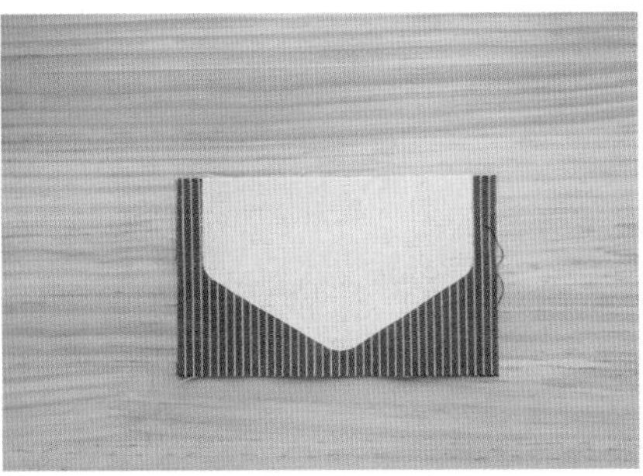

01. Align the interfacing on the top edge of the outer fabric top layer. The outer fabric does not need a seam allowance for the top edge.

02. On the top edge of the lining fabric for the bottom layer, leave a ¼" (0.5cm) seam allowance.

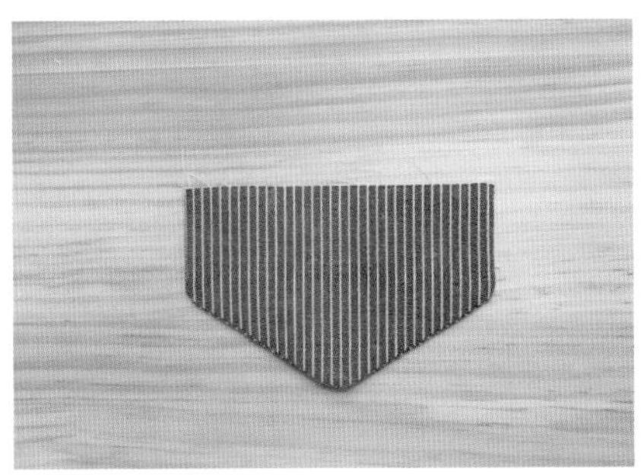

03. Place the top layer fabrics together with right sides facing and sew a seam around the edges. Clip the seam allowances with pinking shears and turn the fabric right side out. Apply the lace medallion called for in your pattern if applicable.

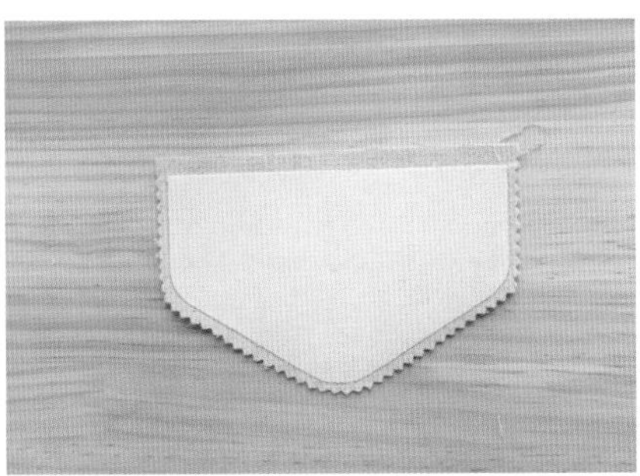

04. Follow the same instructions for the bottom layer fabric pieces.

05. Line up the top layer over the bottom layer of fabric (tuck the monogrammed ribbon in between if your project includes it) and edge stitch around the top layer to join them together. Attach the magnetic button if applicable.

06. Line up the flap on the main body of the bag and sew a seam just outside the outer fabric to join the fabric together.

07. Lift up the flap and sew a seam with a 5⁄16" (0.7cm) seam allowance.

08. Your flap is complete!

B: Flat Bag Flaps

Version 1: Single Layer Flap: 2 pieces of fabric (outer fabric and lining)

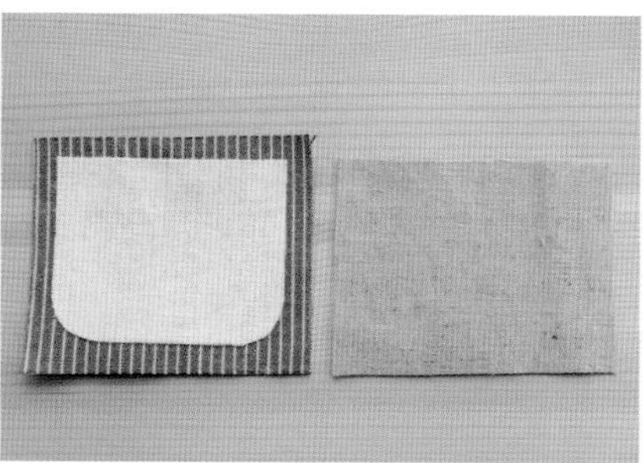

01. When applying the interfacing, note that the outer fabric should have a ¼" (0.5cm) seam allowance along the top edge, while the lining fabric needs no seam allowance along the top edge.

02. Layer the outer fabric and lining together with right sides facing and sew them together along the side and bottom edges.

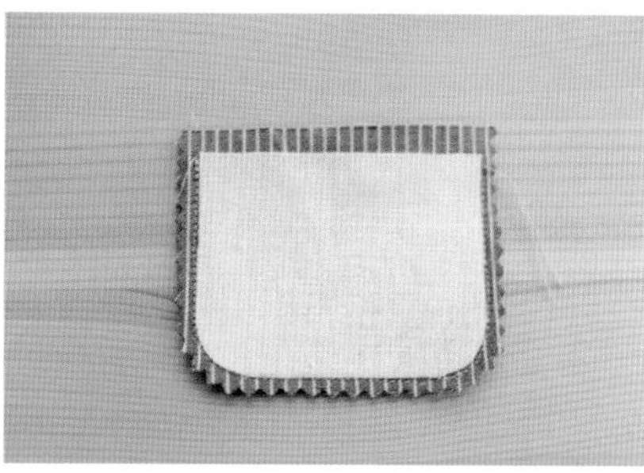

03. Trim the edges with pinking shears, this will make the shape of the flap look better.

04. Turn the flap right side out and iron it. Edge stitch around the edges to secure it. Note how the outer fabric extends beyond the lining.

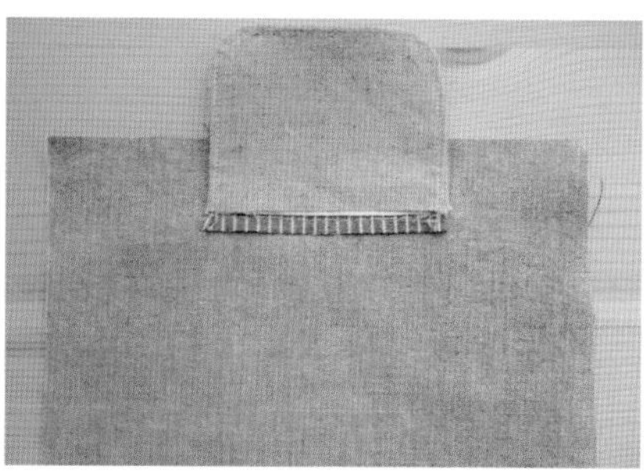

05. Place the flap on the main fabric of the bag with right sides facing each other. Sew a seam just outside the edge of the lining fabric.

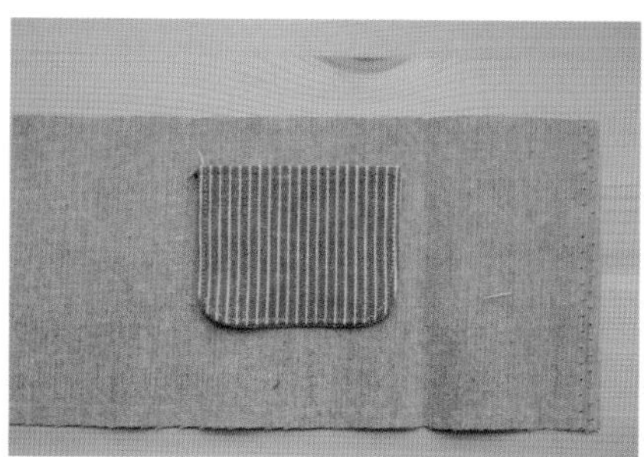

06. Fold the flap bag down, and sew another seam 5⁄16" (0.7cm) down from the folded edge to finish the flap.

Version 2: Double-Layered Flap: A total of four pieces of fabric (top layer outer fabric and lining, bottom layer outer fabric and lining)

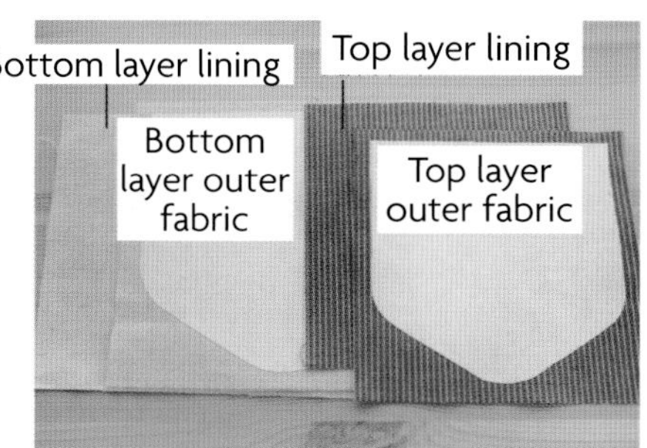

01. Iron the interfacing to the fabric pieces. The top layer outer fabric, lining, and bottom layer outer fabric need a ¼" (0.5cm) seam allowance along the top edge.

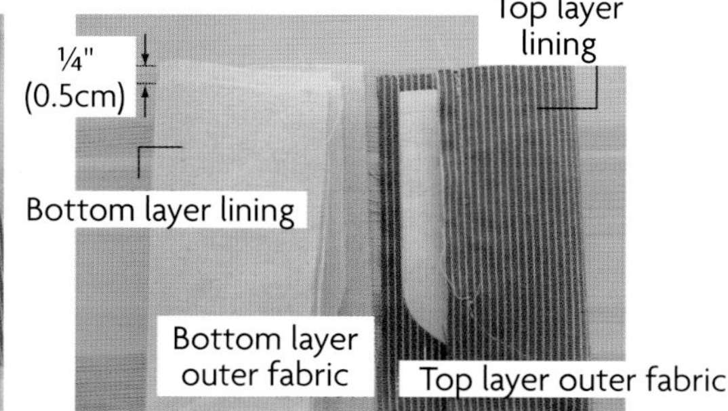

02. Line up the top layer outer fabric and lining together with right sides facing and sew a seam around the side and bottom edges to join them. Repeat this with the bottom layers of fabric.

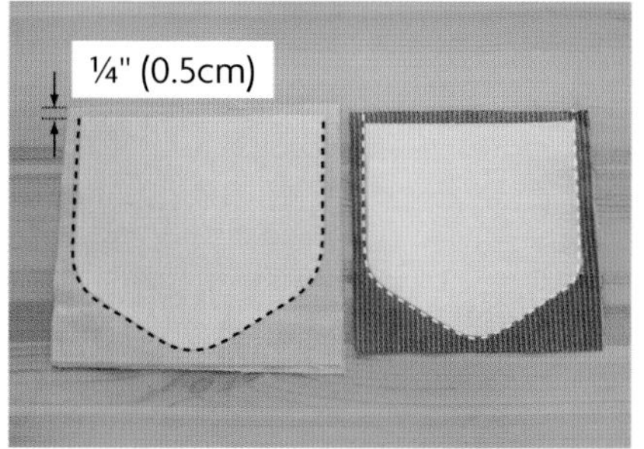

03. Note how the outer fabric of the bottom layer extends beyond the lining.

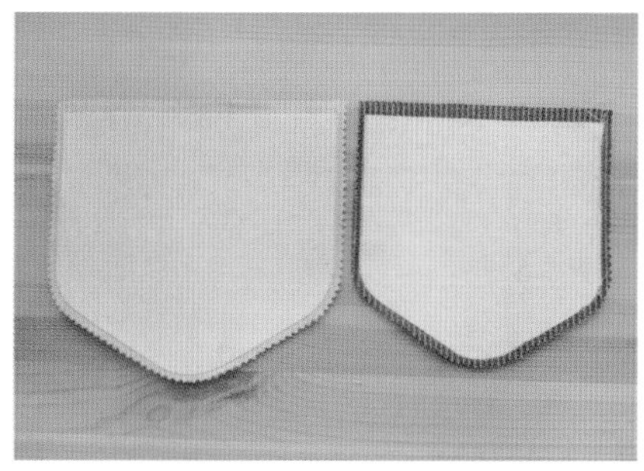

04. Trim the seam allowances with pinking shears.

05. Turn the fabric right side out and iron it. Apply the decorative lace medallion to the top layer (if the project includes it) and edge stitch along the edges of the bottom layer of fabric.

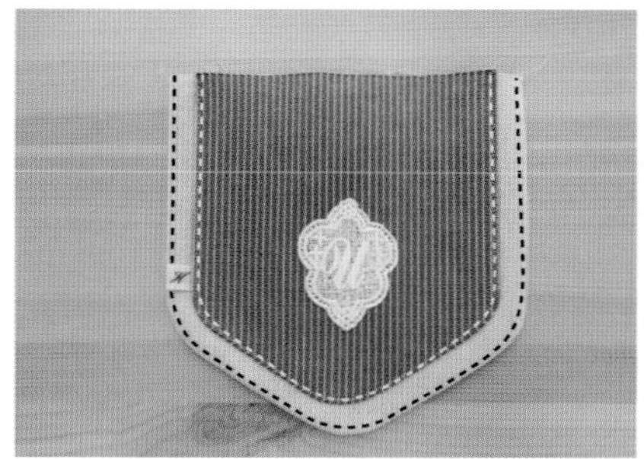

06. Align the top layer onto the bottom layer (tuck the monogrammed ribbon in between if your project includes it) and edge stitch the top layer in place. Attach the magnetic snap to the flap.

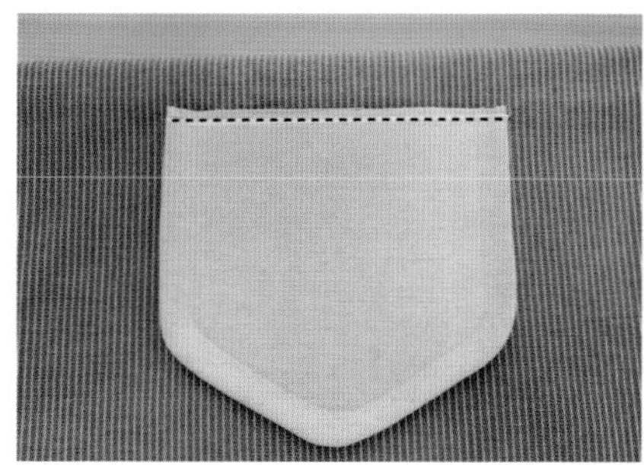

07. Place the flap on the main fabric with right sides facing and sew a seam on the edge of the interfacing, just outside the lining fabric.

08. Lift up the flap and sew it in place 5⁄16" (0.7cm) from the folded edge to finish the flap.

C: Compartment Pockets

Version 1: Total of One Piece of Fabric: inner and outer fabric as the same piece

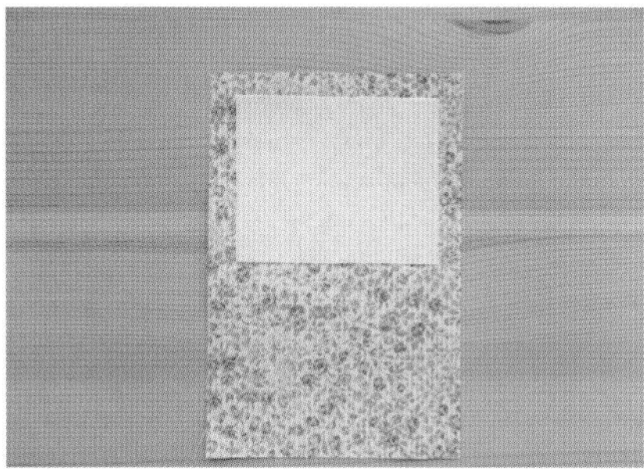

01. Iron the interfacing onto what will be the outside of the pocket. The interfacing does not require a seam allowance.

02. Fold the fabric in half with right sides facing so the bottom edge meets the top edge. Sew a seam along the sides, leaving a small opening at the top.

03. Iron the seam and trim the four corners, being sure not to cut the bottom.

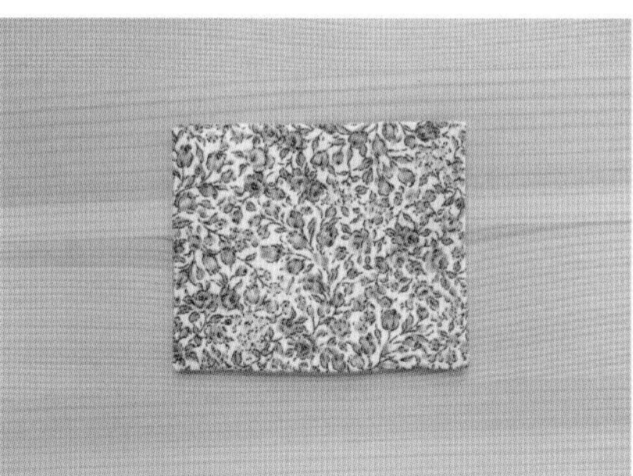

04. Turn the fabric right side out and iron it. Sew a seam along the top edge of the pocket.

05. Align the pocket wherever you would like to place it, and sew a seam around the sides and bottom to set it in place. On the top two edges you can sew a triangle-shaped seam to make the pocket more secure.

Version 2: Total of Two Pieces of Fabric: separate fabrics for the outside and inner pocket

01. Iron the interfacing to the fabric that will be the outer pocket, positioning it in the center. Make sure to leave seam allowances on all four sides of the fabric.

02. Place the outer pocket and pocket lining fabrics together with front sides facing. Sew a seam along all the edges, leaving a small opening in one side.

03. Iron the seam and trim the four corners, making sure not to cut the seams.

04. Turn the fabric right side out and iron it. Sew a seam along the top edge.

05. Line up the pocket on the main fabric and sew a seam around the side and bottom edges.

Version 3: Pocket sewn directly onto the main fabric of the bag

01. Iron the interfacing onto what will be the outside pocket. Place the interfacing aligned with the center of the fabric.

02. Fold down the top edge of the fabric to meet the bottom edge with wrong sides together and iron it. Edge stitch along the fold.

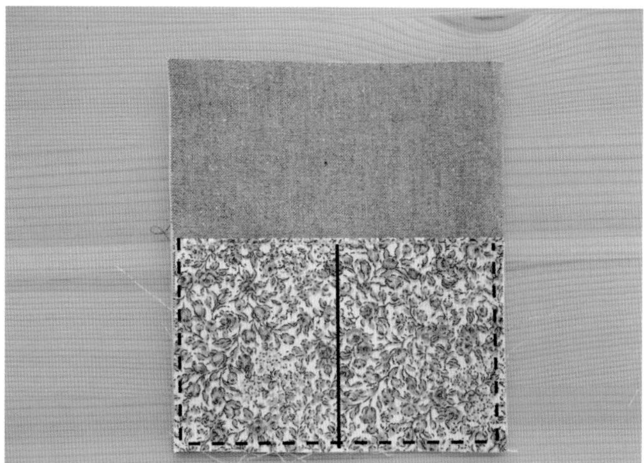

03. Line up the pocket on the bag's main fabric and baste it in place along the bottom and side edges. If needed, you can also sew a seam down the center of the pocket in order to create separate compartments.

D: Three-Dimensional Pockets

Version 1: Sewn onto the center of the main body of the bag

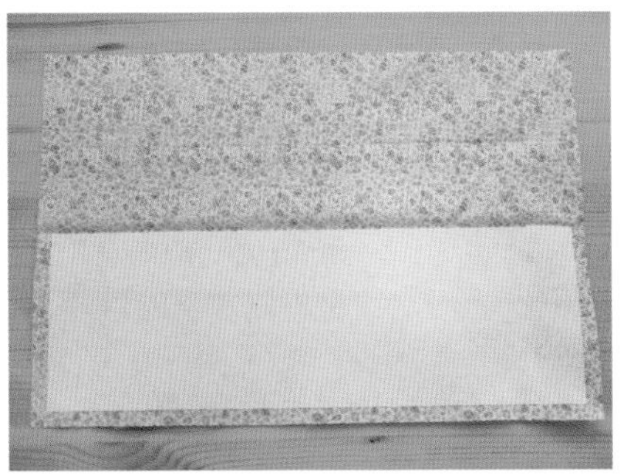

01. Iron the interfacing onto what will be the outer pocket fabric. Line up the interfacing along the center line.

02. Fold down the top edge to meet the bottom edge with right sides together and sew a seam along the side and bottom edges. Be sure to leave an opening along the bottom edge.

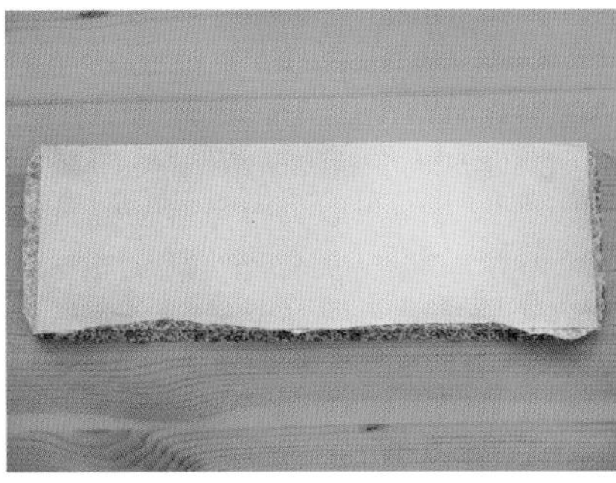

03. Trim the four corners and iron the seam.

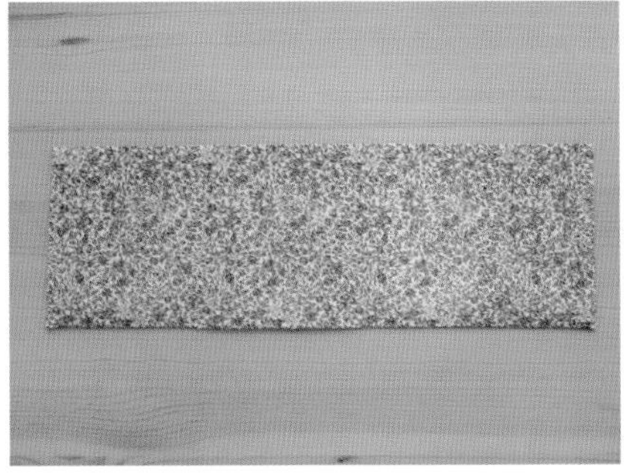

04. Turn the pocket right side out and iron it. Make the marks required by the project directions or according to your specific needs.

05. Along each fold line, sew a pin tuck.

06. The finished pocket will resemble a ⊓ shape.

07. Layer the finished pocket over the main fabric of the bag, folding together the pin tucks to create the inverted pleats that will be your three-dimensional sections. Sew the pocket in place along the sides and bottom edges as well as the marked separation lines.

08. You have completed your three-dimensional pocket.

Version 2: Sewn directly onto the main fabric of the bag

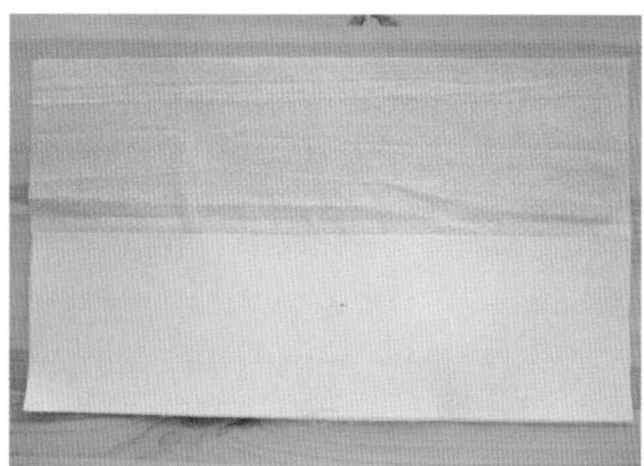

01. First iron the interfacing onto what will be the outer pocket fabric. Align the interfacing along the center folding line.

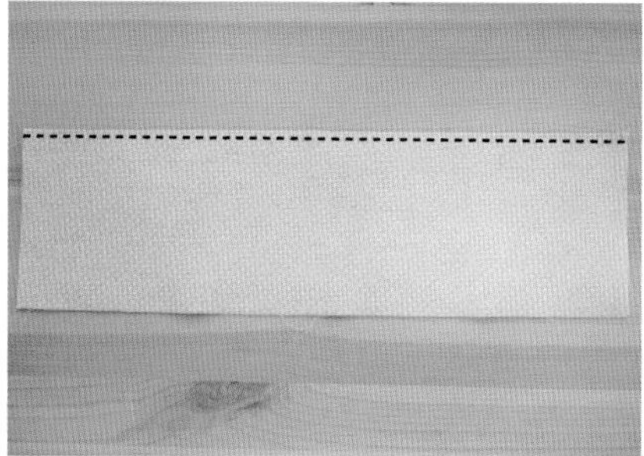

02. Fold the top edge down to meet the bottom edge and iron the fabric. Edge stitch along the top edge of the fold to secure it.

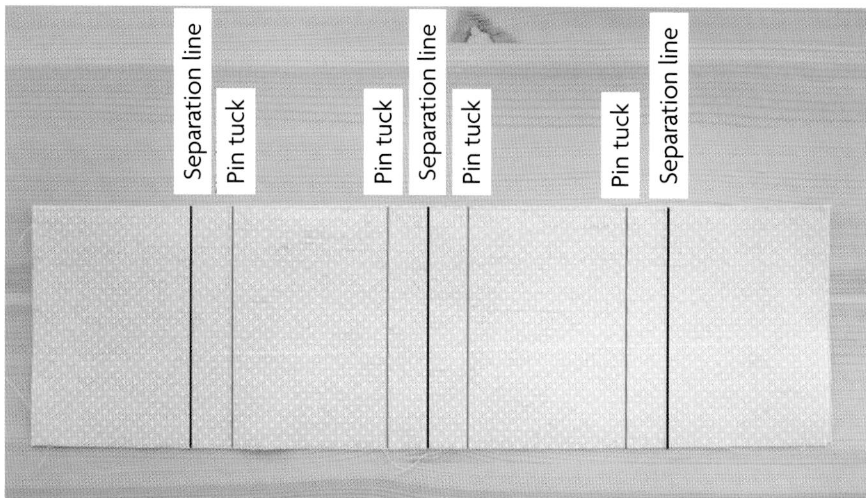

03. According to the project instructions, mark the placement of the pin tuck lines and separation lines.

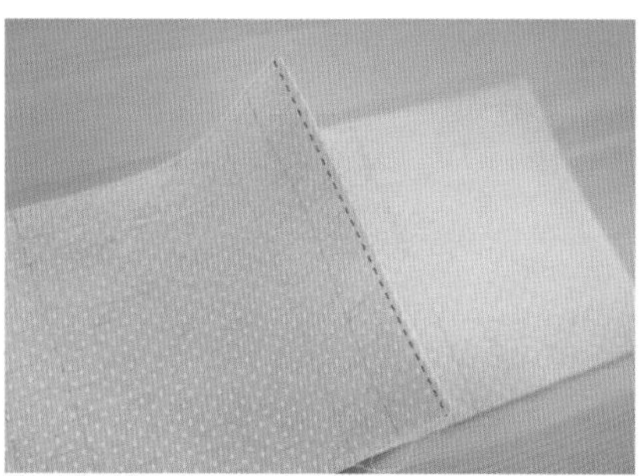

04. Fold the fabric up along these pin tuck lines and sew a pin tuck there.

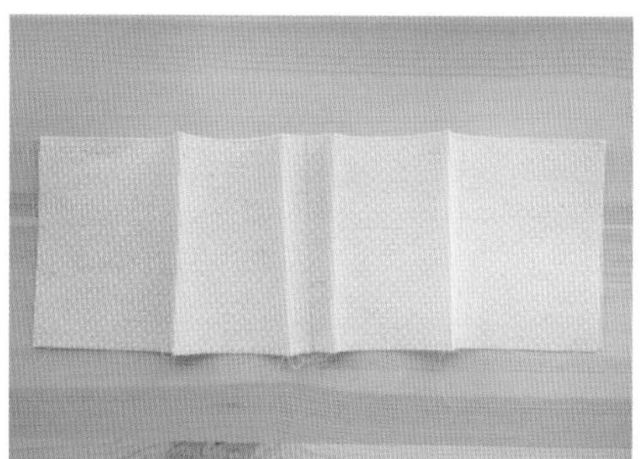

05. The finished pocket will resemble a ⎍ shape.

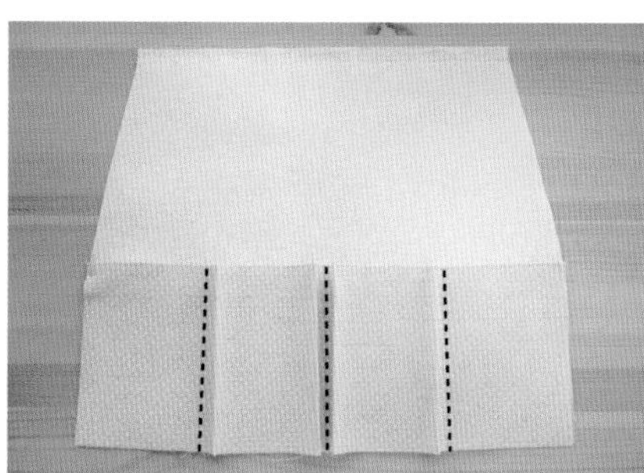

06. Lay the pocket onto the main fabric of the bag and fold the pin tucks in place to create the three-dimensional sections. Sew seams along the sides and bottom as well as the separation lines to finish your pocket.

E: Elastic Pockets

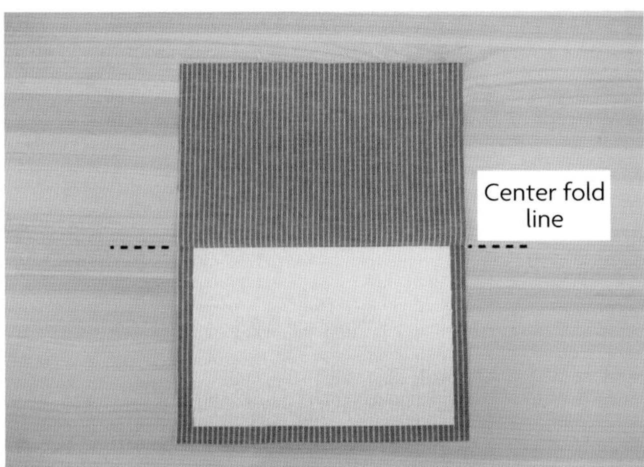

01. First iron the interfacing onto what will be the outer pocket fabric, making sure to line up the interfacing along the center fold line of the fabric.

02. Fold the top edge of the fabric towards the bottom edge and iron it flat. Sew two seams along the top edge of the fabric, first an edge stitch close to the fold, then another seam ⅜" (1cm) from the previous seam. The width here depends on the width of the elastic you choose.

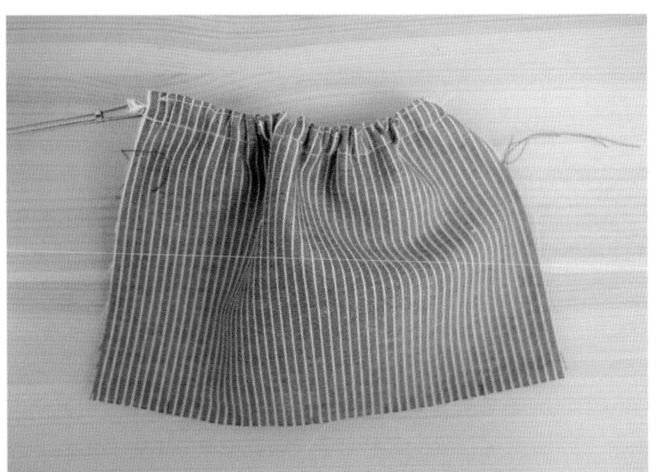

03. Thread the elastic through the channel you've just sewn, then baste the elastic ends in place as it is guided through.

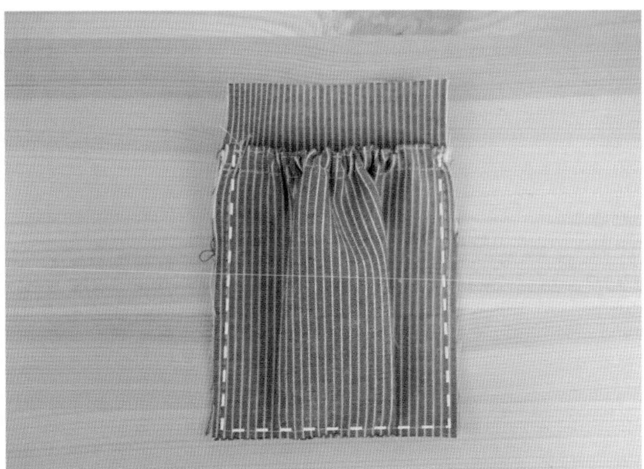

04. Align the pocket onto the main fabric for the bag, make any pleats in the pocket as the project requires, and baste it in place along the side and bottom edges.

F: Zipper Pockets

01. Iron the interfacing to the pocket fabric. Mark the placement lines for the zipper opening. Layer the pocket fabric over the main bag fabric with right sides facing and use pins to hold it in place.

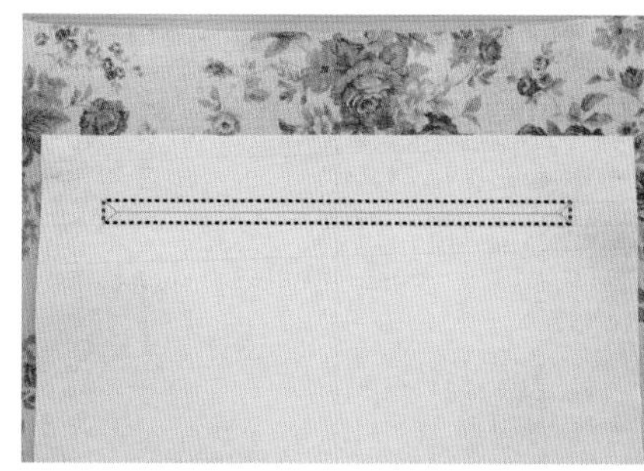

02. Sew a seam around the rectangle that forms the zipper opening.

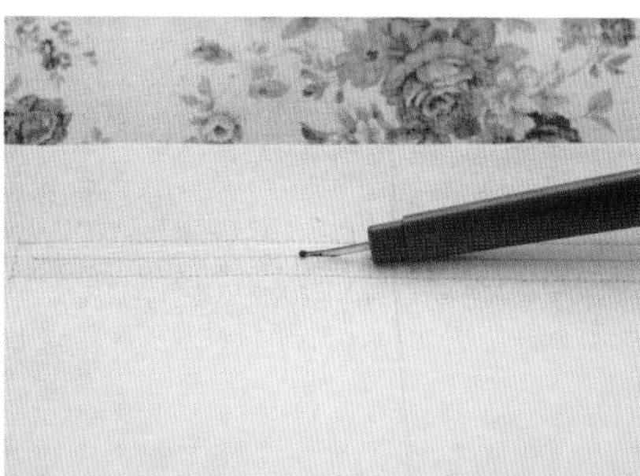

03. Use a seam ripper to start to open up the zipper opening.

04. Use scissors to cut open the rest of the opening, cutting along the marks as close as possible to the seam without cutting through it.

05. Open up the small flaps you've just cut and iron them flat.

06. Feed the pocket fabric through the opening.

07. Turn the pocket fabric to the other side and iron it flat.

08. Use fusible web to anchor the zipper in place onto the back side of the fabric while you sew it. Edge stitch completely around the opening to anchor the zipper in place.

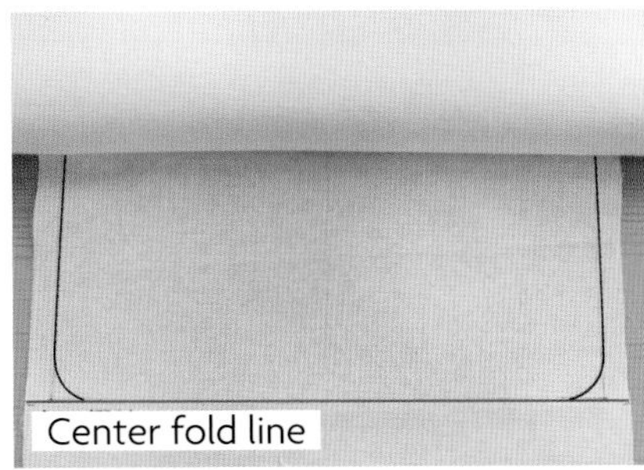

09. Fold the bottom edge of the pocket up to meet the top edge. Draw rounded corners along the bottom side seams.

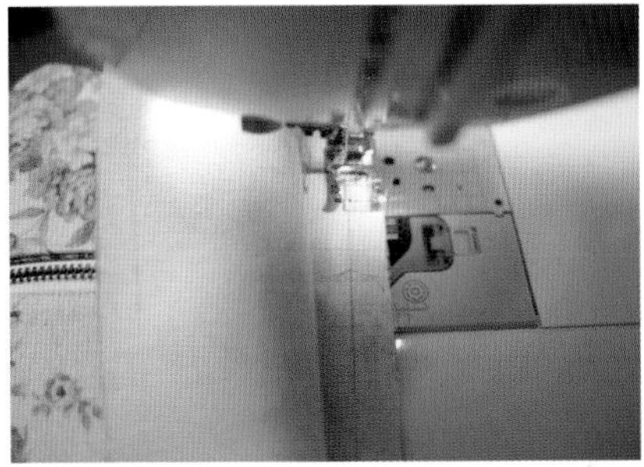

10. Sew the edges of the pocket fabric together, lifting up the sides of the outer fabric if it gets in the way.

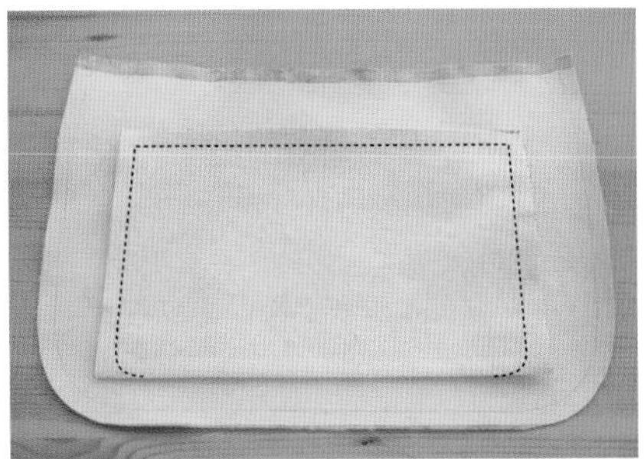

11. The sewn edges of the pocket fabric should resemble this.

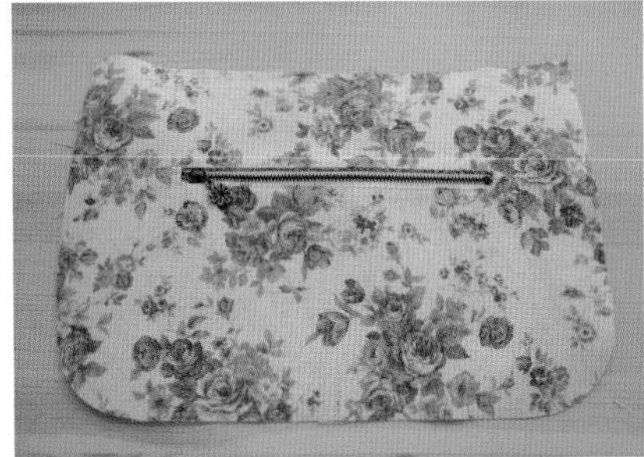

12. You have now finished your zipper pocket.

G: Purse Feet

01. Purse feet come in all different shapes and sizes, so choose your feet according to the measurements of the product that you are making in order to find feet which best suit your bag.

02. Make marks on your plastic board for where you will punch holes for your purse feet. Trim the four corners to make them rounded.

03. Pull your purse fabric around the plastic board and sew a gathering seam to gather the fabric around the edges of the board. Cover the board enough so the plastic won't damage the fabric of your bag.

04. Use a hole punch to make the openings for the purse feet.

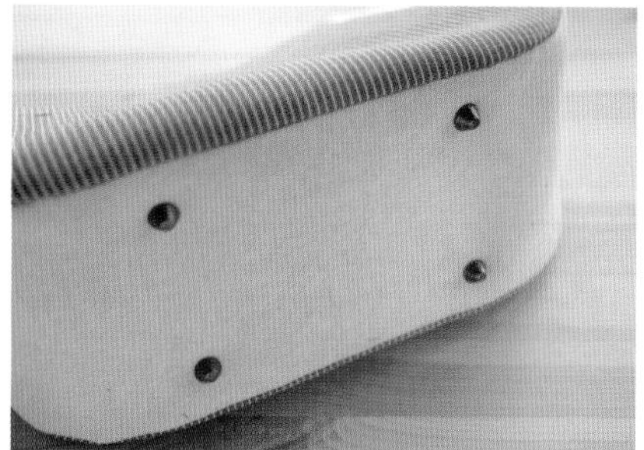

05. Punch holes in the main fabric of the bag. Attach the purse feet from the outside of the bag and pull the prongs through the plastic board.

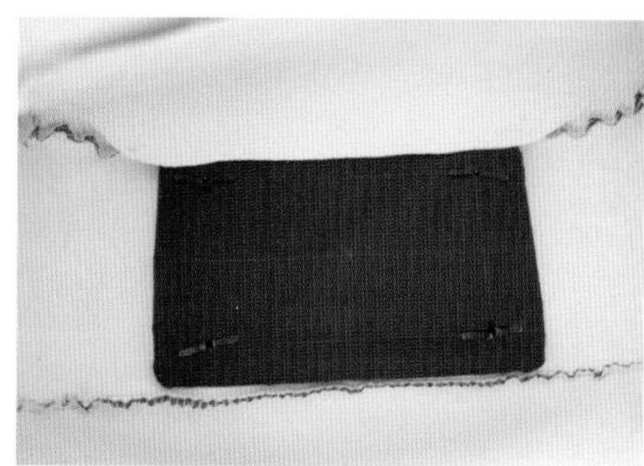

06. If the purse feet have spacers, then pull them through these spacers and then finish attaching them to your plastic board.

H: Wrist Straps

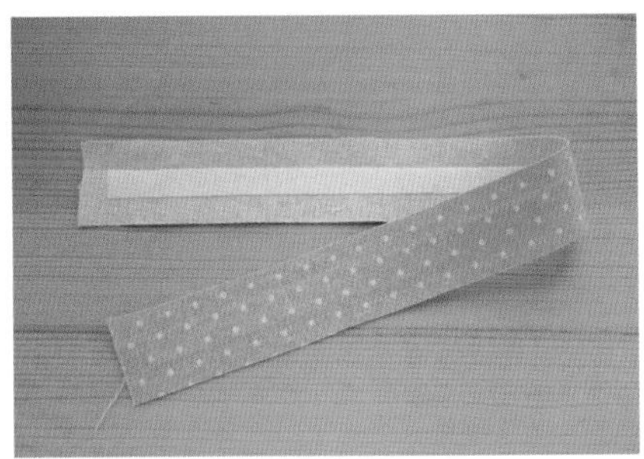

01. To make a 3/8" (1cm) wide strap, trim two pieces of 1⅛" (3cm) wide fabric, and iron a 3/8" (1cm) wide strip of interfacing onto the center.

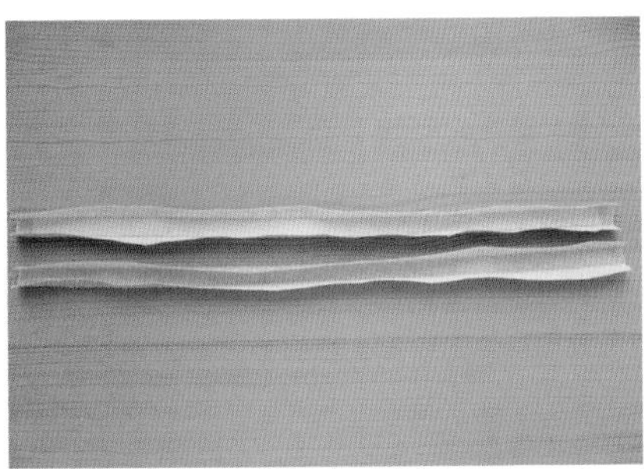

02. Fold under 3/8" (1cm) on each long side of the strap and iron the folds down.

03. Layer the two pieces together with right sides facing, and sew them together along one long side. Open the fabric out and iron the seam.

04. Slide the D-ring onto the strap, then sew the two pieces together along each short end, creating a ring.

05. Fold the fabric back together so the right side is facing outward and iron the strap flat. Use strong clips to hold the folds together and fasten it in place.

06. Edge stitch along each side to secure the strap.

07. Punch two holes in the strap about 1½" (4cm) away from each other with the D-ring in the middle.

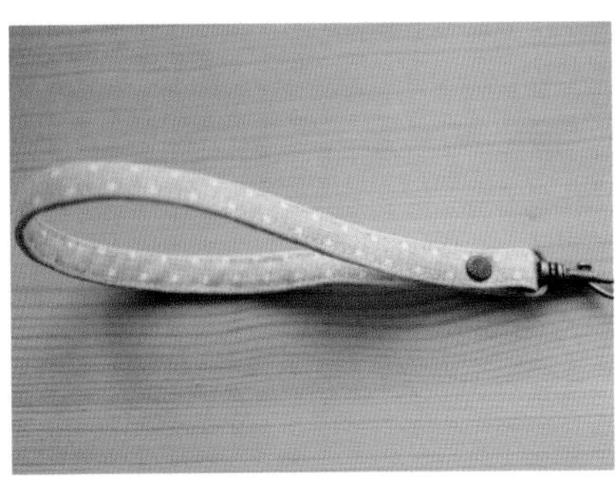

08. Attach a metal rivet here to finish your strap.

I: Shoulder Straps

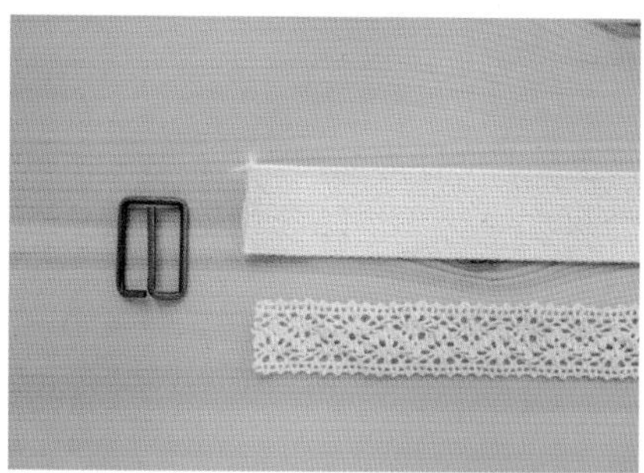

01. If you would like to use decorative lace in your strap, first sew it onto complementing webbing or similar strap material.

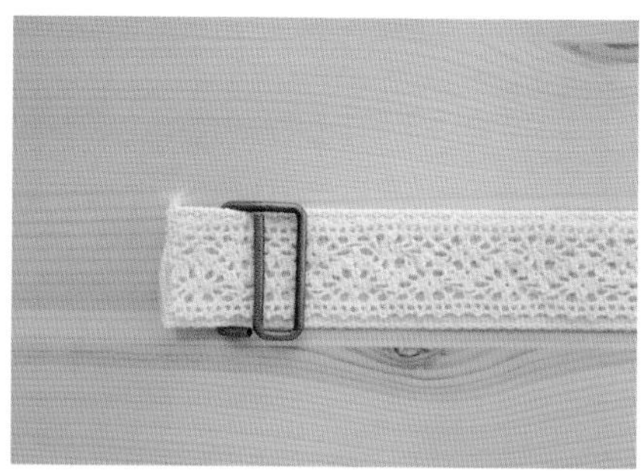

02. Slide the strap through the strap adjuster from the left side.

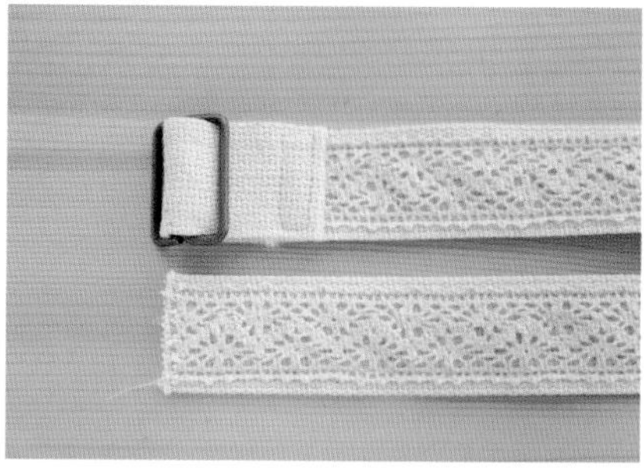

03. Loop the fabric through the adjuster, and fold under the edge twice. Sew the folds in place with a box stitch.

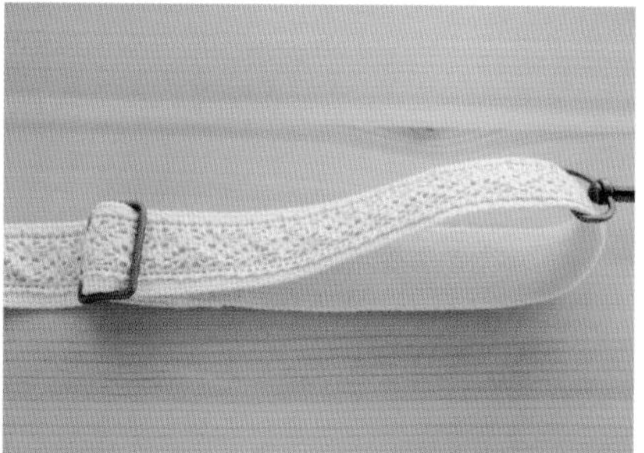

04. From the other end of the strap, slide on the hook ring, then loop the strap through the strap adjuster again.

05. With the remaining raw end, loop it through a second hook ring, then fold under the fabric twice and sew it in place with a box stitch.

J: Leather-Bordered Labels

01. Fold under the sides of the cotton label and iron it flat. Roughly cut a piece of leather larger than the cotton label.

02. Layer the cotton label over the leather and edge stitch it in place.

03. Trim the leather near the edges of the cotton fabric to finish your label.

K: Bias Binding

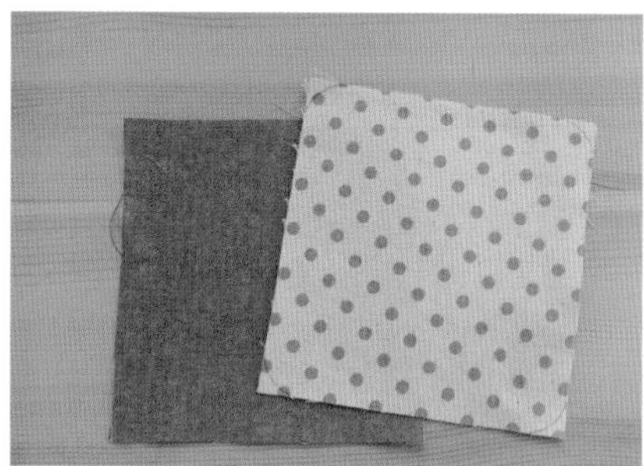

01. Prepare the outer fabric and lining.

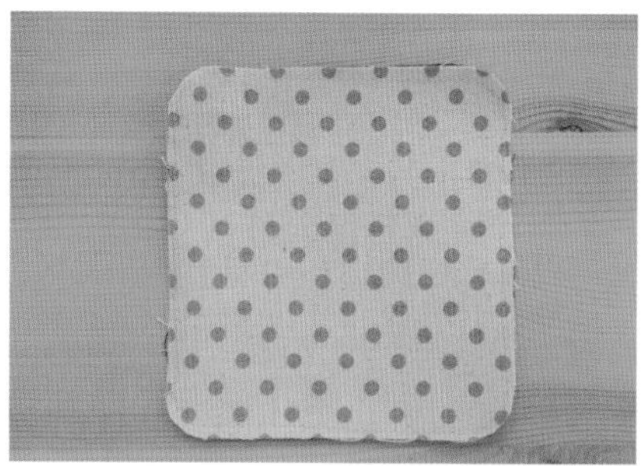

02. Layer them together with wrong sides facing and baste them together around the raw edges.

03. Use a bias tape maker to fold your bias strip of fabric. Iron the folds in place.

04. Line up one fold of the bias tape around the perimeter of your main fabric. Fold under the beginning edge of the tape by ⅜" (1cm), then sew it in place around the fabric, overlapping the ending edge of the tape over the beginning by ⅜" (1cm) when you make it all the way around.

05. Wrap the bias tape around the edge of the main fabric, bringing the second fold to the other side. Iron the fold in place, then sew around the edges once again to finish the border.

L: Piping

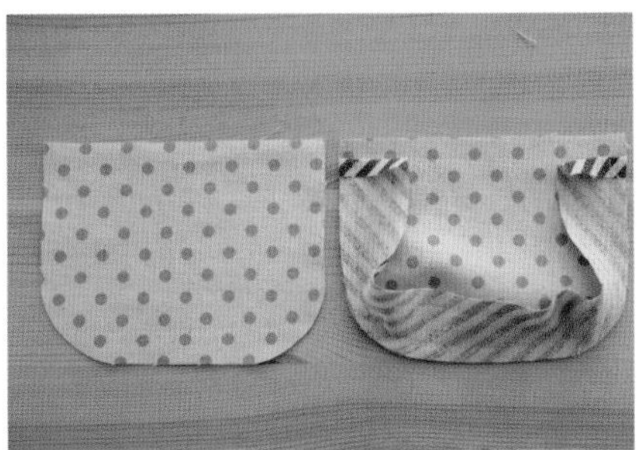

01. Take a strip of bias fabric and fold the two short edges under by ⅜" (1cm). Baste one long edge to your outer fabric.

02. Layer a piece of twine or cotton cord inside the bias strip, then wrap the fabric around the cording, folding it in half. Baste the fold in place along the edge of the main fabric.

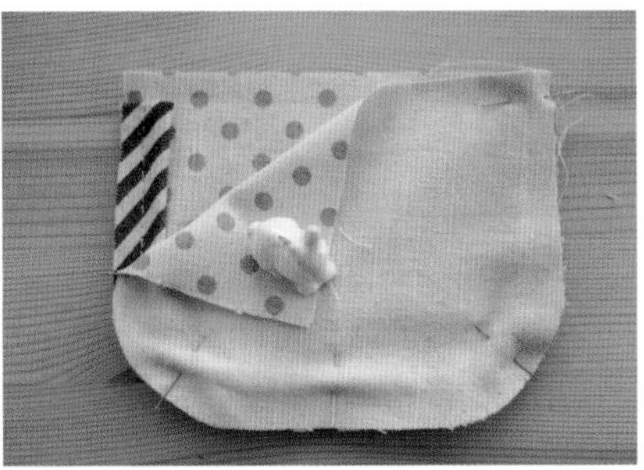

03. Layer the lining fabric over the outer fabric and pin it in place, matching up the edges.

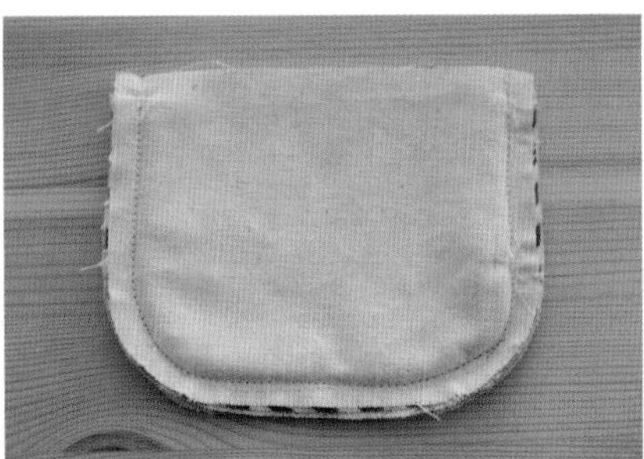

04. Sew the seam as before, using a zipper foot to sew as close as possible to the cording.

05. Trim the seam allowances at the corners and turn the fabric right side out. Your piping is now finished.

M: Magnetic Snaps and Push-Lock Clasps

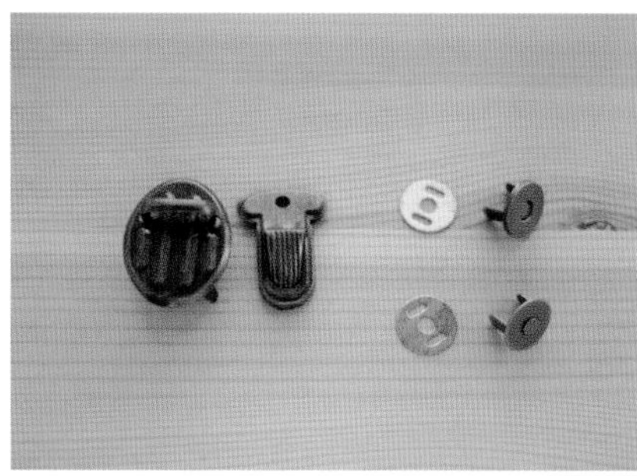

01. The application of magnetic snaps and push-locks should be the same and they should all have base backings.

02. First determine in advance the placement of the snap by making crosshair marks on the fabric. Draw the placement mark for the base of the snap using the spacer.

03. Use a seam ripper to cut an opening for the base.

04. Insert the base of the magnetic snap into the opening.

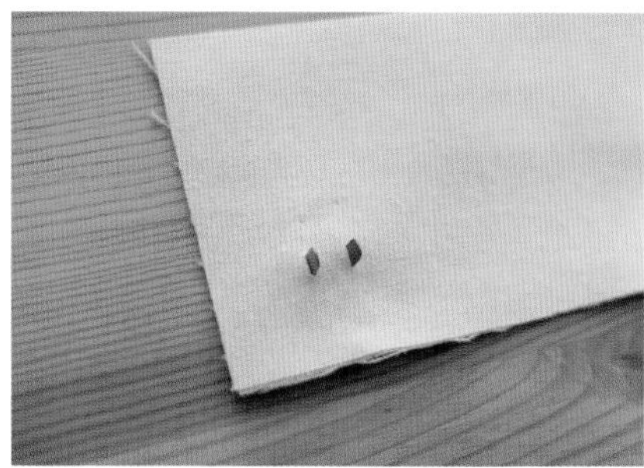

05. The snap should look like the picture when viewed from the back.

06. Attach the spacer onto the snap base, then bend the prongs evenly outward.

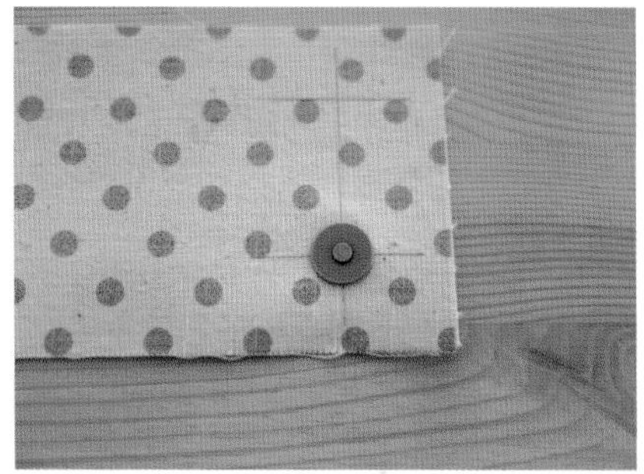

07. Now you have finished your magnetic snap.

Index

More Pretty Little Things from Cherie Lee

If you love the simple elegance of Sewing Pretty Little Accessories, you'll be glad to hear there's more to make! Cherie Lee's first book from Design Originals offers even more exquisite accessories for you to sew, using just fabric remnants and little scraps of cloth.

In her first book, Cherie shows you how to give new purpose to special pieces of material by transforming them into a variety of wonderful purses and bags—from evening bags, clutches, and coin purses to backpacks, tote bags, and more. You'll discover imaginative ideas for making useful items and meaningful gifts featuring her classic, beautiful designs.

ISBN 978-1-57421-611-0 **$19.99**
DO5301

Look for Cherie Lee's first volume at your local bookstore or specialty retailer, or at d-originals.com

Galeries St Martin
Paris

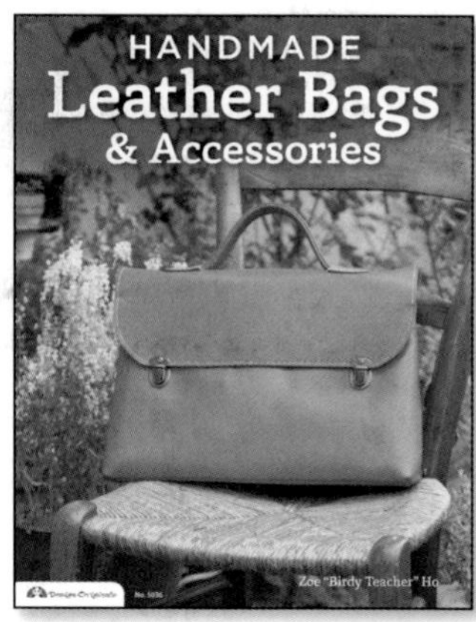

Handmade Leather Bags & Accessories
ISBN 978-1-57421-716-2 **$19.99**
DO5036

Sewing Stylish Handbags & Totes
ISBN 978-1-57421-422-2 **$22.99**
DO5393

Sew Me! Sewing Basics
ISBN 978-1-57421-423-9 **$19.99**
DO5394

Sew Me! Sewing Home Décor
ISBN 978-1-57421-504-5 **$14.99**
DO5425

Sewing Leather Accessories
ISBN 978-1-57421-623-3 **$14.99**
DO5313

Making Clothes for Your Dog
ISBN 978-1-57421-610-3 **$19.99**
DO5300

Sew Fun for Girls & Dolls
ISBN 978-1-57421-364-5 **$11.99**
DO3487

Seaside Quilts
ISBN 978-1-57421-431-4 **$24.99**
DO5402

Soft Toys
ISBN 978-1-57421-501-4 **$9.99**
DO5422

Look for These Books at Your Local Bookstore or Specialty Retailer or at *www.D-Originals.com*